# THE SOLENT AND THE SOUTHERN WATERS

TO THE NEEDLES

# THE SOLENT AND THE SOUTHERN

WATERS A Casual Exploration
of the Seaways about the Isle of Wight and of the
Creeks and Inlets from Chichester to Poole, by
H. ALKER TRIPP ("LEIGH HOE")
ILLUSTRATED BY THE AUTHOR

**CONWAY MARITIME PRESS**
**GREENWICH**

First Edition 1928
Second Edition 1973
**Published by** Conway Maritime Press Ltd
7 Nelson road, Greenwich, London
SE 10
**ISBN** 0 85177 064 9

Printed in Great Britain by
Unwin Brothers Ltd., Old Woking, Surrey

50 11

# FOREWORD

THE English country-side has a whole literature of its own ; its lanes have been explored, its topography examined, and its landscape described in books without number.

The coastal seaways and creeks deserve their own notice too. The present writer—now for the third time—has sought to apply to the home seaways the same ideas of exploration as have been so often and so happily applied by others to the highways and byways ashore.

The illustrations are from sketches made mostly afloat—sketches in which horizons were wobbly sometimes from the tumble of the home seaways.

The small ship of these pilgrimages is *Growler*, a twelve-ton yacht of barge type, cutter-rigged, built at Maldon, Essex. After the modern fashion, *Growler* has an auxiliary engine now, but the engine was not yet in commission during the voyages described. They were made under sail.

# CONTENTS

ix

# LIST OF ILLUSTRATIONS

## IN MONOCHROME

## IN LINE

# LIST OF ILLUSTRATIONS xiii

# THE SOLENT AND THE SOUTHERN WATERS

# CHAPTER I

## OUT OF LONDON AGAIN

EVERY new voyage is a new adventure, and we went on board at Wapping with as much exhilaration as if we had never embarked before. However modest the expedition, the same sense is there :

> Beyond the East the sunrise, beyond the West the sea,
> And East and West the wander thirst that will not let me be.

So we stowed the bread in the bin, saw that the tanks of drinking water were full, uncorded the bale of groceries, and generally made ready. The yacht lay steadily enough here, save when some passing tug set her rolling ; and, as I steadied myself from the roll, I remembered that the shelves in the cabin had not yet been cleared, and things below made properly fast. A salt-water passage, though it be but a couple of hundred miles, is apt to give its diverse samples of weather. And this roll from the tugs was a mild business compared with the tumble of a turn to windward off the South Foreland or Beachy Head. The *hit* of the breaking waves upon her bows shakes the yacht all through ; it is apt to make an unholy mess below if anything is left loose in the cabin.

This was not a bad starting-point for us—under sail from beside old Wapping Stairs, for the fame of Wapping Stairs belongs entirely to the days of sail. Generations of boatmen loitered here, ready to put passengers on board the sailing packets in mid-stream ; and the traveller can still hail a waterman much as he hails a cabman ashore. But the whole scene has been changed out of recognition ; not only have the square-riggers gone, but the old houses have mostly disappeared, and Execution Dock has gone altogether—the place where pirates were hung and sun-dried, their bodies dangling in chains. Everything is altered ; massive steel shipping and mighty cranes and miles of dockland form the picture now in this modern Port of London.

The tide had turned an hour or more ago, and we were ready. We cast off the warps. As the yacht filled away on her sunlit mainsail, the riverside front of Wapping slid from her. The sense of movement, in this quiet water, was smoothness itself. She was away.

The hours of high tide are always busy, and the river traffic was congested. Past Shadwell and Ratcliff a very heedful course had to be threaded. The entrance to Limehouse Basin lay on the north side of us, and the Surrey Commercial Docks on the south. Tugs and barges were everywhere, and the moored ships towered among them.

A big freighter was moving slowly in mid-stream,

and I had been eyeing her movements with some suspicion as we swept towards her, running free with the ebb.

"Three hoots—she's going astern!" I called. Her propeller, half out of the water, was thrashing up a lather of foam ; and, on the other side of us, just at the moment, a tug with a string of lighters was butting upstream. The tug sent us a wash with something of a kick in it, so that things were noisy and congested for the moment. Some other steamer—like a cliff of steel with derricks above— had taken all our wind. But the tide sucked us through. Then a fresher puff came, and we were out of it all.

"Gybe-oh! Mind your head!" Here was Greenwich, and at bottom of that U curve round the Isle of Dogs the main-boom must be squared away on the other side. The mainsheet was shortened, and the sail went over with a *thud*.

These place-names of the river are full of suggestion. One must not linger over them here. But, bound as the yacht now was Solent-way, a reference to Greenwich is excusable. Henry VIII and Elizabeth were both born at the Royal Palace, and both sovereigns changed the local fortunes of the Hampshire waterside. Henry VIII created the modern significance of Portsmouth, diverting to it the old naval activity of Southampton ; Elizabeth preferred the Thames to either. Deptford (which we had just passed) was her royal dockyard, and here the *Golden Hind* came home, after sailing round the world.

Though deadened somewhat by London smoke, the sunlight was bright enough to-day, and the going was good. The sailing barges, with their tall topsails, were getting a fuller breeze than our own, for a trio of them—sailing in company—had maintained their lead on us. But the stumpies, needless to say, could not. More than one stumpy, sighted far ahead, was gradually overhauled, and was dropped into the smoky distance astern.

Much though the river may change, the sailing barges are unaltered. They sailed here when the old East Indiamen were built at Blackwall, and when the collier brigs were here, those little brigs which used sometimes to beat up in such close company as almost to make the waterway solid with them. The Blackwall frigates and collier brigs are gone ; the barges remain.

The docks of London, more and more during the last century or so, have taken the larger shipping out of sight, and hidden it from the passer-by who sails down the river. All the ships at one time lay crowded beside the fairway, three-deep or more. Now the big ships are stowed away somewhere in a vague background of docks, clear of the stream.

" Two great funnels there "—and I pointed over the roofs and chimneys—" a big ship, that."

Masts and funnels crop up like this, here and there, above the warehouses and cranes alongshore and over the chimney-tops ; but much is lost to sight entirely.

Erith was passed, and Erith Rands. Through Long Reach the ebb still carried us, but the wind was less vigorous. Would it push us over the tide when the flood, like a mill-race, came sluicing in from seaward, against us ? I began to have my doubts. As we slid by Greenhithe (where the old " hithe " or quay is still as picturesque as ever), I looked down at the cabin clock.

" The ebb will be finished in an hour ; there's a good berth over there " (and I pointed across the Northfleet Hope to a spot below the *Exmouth*). " I've brought up here before now. It may come to that to-day ; we may have to anchor for the six hours of foul tide."

Off Broadness, when we reached it, the tide was slackening, almost on the turn. Every stitch of sail that the yacht could muster had been set. Gradually she slid through the Northfleet Hope, and was steered towards the Tilbury shore in order to clear the crowd of anchored vessels on the Gravesend side, and also to cheat the tide. Gradually, gradually still, she clove her way onward through the flood that gurgled and cluttered past ; but more, more, more that strong run of it was checking her. There are huge piles planted well out into the fairway on this side, and beside them we hung poised ; the tide was now racing Londonward in a torrent, and the wind just sufficed to hold us against it— just sufficed and no more. One great upright baulk of timber was on our beam, a few yards away, and there we stopped. The water raced through the whole pile system, with a suck and a gurgle—a heavy scour. The position was distinctly uncomfortable. " Suppose the tide took command and put us in

among those piles ? " I cheerfully surmised. " Look
at all those ties. The mast couldn't pass under
them. Imagine it ! *What* a mess ! "

We disliked the situation ; we frankly did. Now
gaining a little with a puff of breeze, and now
slipping sternwise again, we hung and waited for
more than half an hour.

A French steamer, which had been thrusting
solidly along in mid-channel, turned suddenly and
entered the dock just ahead of us, taking the entrance
at a surprising speed. Her wash, and the wash of
tugs and passing ships, set us a-roll and a-joggle in
our awkward suspension. This did not add to our
comfort, and it was a relief when the wind again
freshened, so that we really began to creep seaward
once more.

These small anxieties, once over, only served to
put a finer edge on pleasure when, in a golden
afternoon, we left the congestion of Tilbury and
Gravesend astern of us. Having gained the Ovens
Spit (and course was laid across it, cheating the
tide), we felt a sense of escape.

" Let the wind drop now, or let it breeze up," I
said happily ; " it can do as it jolly well likes. We
don't care two hoots. There's plenty of room."

Day was nearly over ; and, as five hours of contrary tide were still before us, we hoped of course
that the freshening breeze would decide to hold.
It might peter out at nightfall. From golden sunlight in the Lower Hope, we passed to sunset soon
after we had opened Sea Reach. The change came
very quickly over the spirit of everything, and the

seascape was coloured with the cold grey-blue of the twilight. After reaching down to the Mucking, we had now squared away, and were running free. Over the Blyth Sand, barges and bawleys were bringing up in numbers for the night; sails were being furled everywhere, and riding lights set. The sight of it conjured the idea of a snug supper and a quiet turn-in, a fancy not without its own allurement in this chilly nightfall. But we were outward bound. Waste of the fair wind would be really sinful; and the yacht, with a trusty breeze in her canvas now, swung resolutely on, seaward. Lights began to twinkle from Leigh and Southend, and the steamships showed coloured eyes of green and red as they thrust vigorously by. Our own side-lights had been trimmed and lighted, and were now set in their brackets on the shrouds. Day was finished; this was full night.

The Chapman pile lighthouse was astern, and the next important light would be the Nore.

We had settled with the most perfect naturalness to night conditions. The binnacle was alight, and the cabin lamp also; while the yacht herself seemed (as she always does) to acquire a separate confident personality as she plugged forward into the gloom. She had an air of knowing all about it. I conned her lovingly as I stood at the helm—those sails of hers, dark in the night above, and that little square of the cabin doorway (clear-cut with the light within) below them. Inside, on the cabin table, the chart was spread out; the big parallel rulers and the dividers lay upon it. The doors of the cabin were open, for the lamp itself is beneath the helmsman's line of sight, being shut off by the cabin roof ; and, so long as the direct light does not shine in his eyes, the mere glimmer of warmth dazzles him no more than does the binnacle. He wants his eyesight unimpaired ; for—as often as not —he is look-out as well as helmsman, and he wants eyes in the back of his head as much as in front. We were not showing a white stern-light, but a lamp was kept at hand for the purpose, if need be.

Course had been laid by compass for the Nore. In the jewellery of yellow lights that studded the waterway the light was not yet visible. It would only be a pin-point as yet, gleaming every half minute. But . . . yes, there it was ! The binnacle could be ignored now.

" Pleasanter to steer for a mark than by compass," I confessed. " And less exacting too."

Meanwhile the steamer traffic was incessant, and it needed watching. While we had been still skirting the edge of the Blyth Sand we had been clear of the mid-fairway ; but now, with the Jenkin Swatchway abeam, we were converging with it, in the orthodox steamer-track for the Nore. Ship after ship would rise in the distance, her green and red lights a-shine ; if, as she approached, one of them disappeared, she was passing us safely. If both remained, glaring more and more balefully bright as she mounted into size and shape, then, obviously, look out for her !

Just such a one came up behind us here, full and truly astern.

NIGHT ON LONDON RIVER.

"Look at her," I said, "dead astern, following our very track, and close on us. She hasn't a notion we're here!"

The yacht must have been totally invisible to the look-out of the steamer, for, the moment our stern light was shown, she slewed round with quite a sharp turn to northward before settling down on her new course.

The Nore was soon abeam, and the tangle of fairway lights of the Medway—red and white. The traffic streamed on unabated, but it called for nothing save a strict look-out, and was no anxiety. With the wind free, we could steer as straight a course as any power vessel ; the nuisance is when the yacht is beating, and must be perpetually cutting athwart the course of everything else.

The Girdler would be the next important light, distant about eleven miles ; and by compass again the yacht's course was laid. In a straight line into the open seaways of the night she would carry on, perfectly confident that, in due course, the light would glitter up right over the bowsprit.

One is apt to take so much for granted. Here, in the midnight, it seemed no marvel that the yacht should be able to hold an assured course. Yet the land was lost to sight, and the seaway for the next five and twenty miles would be shoaled on all hands with sandbanks and shingles, the grave of ships.

One takes for granted all our modern safeguards. But apart from the compass, and apart from the patient labour of men who have set up seamarks and seen them washed away, and set up better ones and seen them go too, but have persisted and improved them until they remain, and have lighted them and improved their lighting until each one is separately identifiable and sends a light over miles of sea— apart from all this, think of the patient ages of science behind that chart laid out on the cabin table. Early field surveys ashore must have been difficult enough, though everything was fixed and

solid there ; but, on the sea, the thing must have
seemed nearly hopeless. In the year 3000 B.C. a
map of terrain near the Persian Gulf is said to have
been prepared—a thousand years before Abraham.
Five thousand years of science are behind that chart!

What was the hour now ?   I glanced down at the
cabin clock ; it was midnight. The Girdler had by
this time been sighted some ten miles distant, and
the Red Sand light almost as soon. By half-past
one that ten miles had been wiped out, and the
Light Vessel was close aboard of us ; its great beam,
shining like a searchlight, dazzled one's eyes more
and more. The darkness was simply Egyptian all
the time that the light was obscured.

" Bad as the lights of a car, when you're walking,"
my companion said. " Slick, it's gone. And it
leaves you stone-blind. You feel as if you're
tumbling straight into the ditch."

On the same course as ourselves, the steamers had
been steering straight for the Light Vessel, and
passing it at close quarters. Past the Light Vessel
we also swung. Two steamships which had been
mere smudges in the darkness, noticeable only by
reason of a pin-point or two of white or coloured
light, became ships of Fairyland in a moment. The
searchlight was on them. The wheeling beam of
the Girdler, now behind us, had picked them out
with a wonder of glistening detail on a background
of night. The breeze blew, the light dropped
farther and farther astern, and night was again as
black as ever.

But the tide which had been helping us through

the night was now about to turn against us. Before
we made good the distance to the whistle buoy at
the South Shingles the hostile tide was running
strongly. When we hauled the East Tongue abeam,
the time was half-past three. Course was changed
for the N.E. Spit; and, in a broken seaway, a
seaway of wind-creased water, we drove through the
darkness.

" Dawn. Surely."

Gripping the coaming to steady ourselves as the
vessel rolled, we scanned the sky north-eastward.
On a clear night the first glimpse of dawn is always
that dim tinge of paler blue low along the sea-line,
faint almost beyond recognition; and one likes to
be the first to spot it. Yes, it was there.

After the N.E. Spit we steered on until we cleared
the red sector of the North Foreland lighthouse and
entered the white one. The yacht lurched forward
through the shadows. In the grey glimmer of
dawn twilight, the waves had been seen breaking
along the shallows of the Margate Sand, a detached
shoal some three miles offshore. Red dawn meanwhile was broadening seaward; and later there was
a thin sickle of waning moon upon it. This way
and that the tiller was moved, steering the yacht
towards the North Foreland light, as the low cliff-
line grew bolder over a tumbling seaway, and the
light itself was soon forgotten because day had
begun. The lighthouse and white cliffs were clear
in the dawn. Blow out the binnacle now, and
dowse the side-lights. We stretched our limbs and
yawned—it was daylight once more.

The yacht romped on, giving the land a moderate berth ; the course that she was shaping was for the Gull Stream.  Big, smooth rollers were meeting her, great swells of water that were ridging up from seaward to meet the smaller waves made by the local wind, and the yacht rolled, rolled, rolled.  The sun was now up.  This was splendid going ; we had Ramsgate abeam by half-past six, and the wind held.

I rubbed my hands and said it ; it was good.  But I wished perhaps that I had held my peace, for the wind, even as I spoke, had begun to lose its heart. And the tide had just turned, running hard against us.  After a clinking run so far, we hung poised again, between wind and tide ; in the next three whole hours we made good less than three miles. Then the wind, after coming in one strong puff, blew out completely and was gone.

The pace at which we gathered sternway was ludicrous ; we were sweeping Thamesward again. Down with a splash went the anchor, and there, some three miles offshore, between Ramsgate and the Gull Light Vessel, we brought up.

I went below ; my companion was there already, asleep.  Putting my head out an hour later, I found that the sea had settled down to flat calm, save for the rolling waves that still swelled evenly along it.  The surfaces were like burnished armour, rounded but smooth.  And—despite the strong sunshine—the sensation of colour was silvery rather than golden ; the Ramsgate coastline, with its white cliffs, was a mere ribbon, low on the sealine, and nothing else was present save one immense effect of silveriness and light.

Less than twenty-four hours ago we had been in the heart of the business of Wapping ; smoke had hung about us like a curtain, and the clatter of derricks and the blended murmur of a thousand distant noises had been endless. And now— this !

But not for long is it possible to be anchored in the Downs or the Gull Stream without becoming an object of interest to the hovellers of Deal beach, and the throb-throb-throb of a motor engine disturbed the silence. The men of the Deal galley punts have taken to engines like every one else in these days.

" Tow you anywhere ? "

No, there would be no sense in that. Had we been bound for Dover or Ramsgate in a hurry to catch a train, the boat might have been a godsend. As it was, we had days and nights for nearly a whole week before us. As long as the weather remained calm we were happy here, happier here than in Dover Harbour ; if the wind breezed up from any quarter at all, we should be happier still. " No ; thanks all the same." And the Deal hovellers went, throb-throb-throb, back to Deal, empty-handed.

The tide would turn at two o'clock. I set the alarm for that hour, and went below for a nap.

Wind—I knew—would awaken me. Sure enough, the welcome sound of it broke into my sleep shortly after one. Up I went. The wind was breezing up from the south, a dead-noser here, and the sky was filled with masses of rolling sunlit cloud.

" Rouse out ! " I shouted ; and I had the tiers off the mainsail before my companion had left his bunk.

The wind was increasing every minute, and—blowing as it was straight through the Downs—it had knocked up a hollow breaking sea the moment that the tide turned. *Growler* pounded and thumped through it. With her full shape, she felt the breaking seas to the utmost ; they thudded on her, and she *shook*. The sunshine had gone within an hour, and a grim grey day had succeeded with a wind that gave her all that she wanted under her whole mainsail. We made long boards—to the Gull on the one hand, and in to Deal pier head on the other. The spray flew and the wind whistled—a change indeed !

By the time that we had brought St. Margaret's Bay abeam, the wind had veered a point or two to the westward, heading us again. Progress seemed inordinately slow ; and meanwhile we debated matters to the tune of the thudding seas, with interruptions by a mouthful or two of salt water. Oil-skinned and sou'-westered, we were raked with spray. Should we make Dover, or should we carry on all night ?

We could sleep in turns, of course. But could we ? In a keeled vessel we could. . . . " Then why not in this ? " my companion (on his first voyage in a barge) demanded. " Lee-boards," I answered. " You can't have the board on the weather side flaring away and wrenching this way and that in a rough sea ; and you can't get a lee-board up or lower it down without leaving the tiller and climbing out of the well. The yacht won't take care of herself for one instant without flying into the wind. No, in anything approaching heavy weather at night, she's too much of a handful for one man when she's turning to windward."

We took the wise decision. Into Dover Harbour at seven o'clock in the evening we sailed—a place of peace after the confused seaway outside. Down went the anchor. The tide would be favouring us, coastwise, after 2 a.m., but I manfully forbore to set the alarm clock. I felt that a full night's rest had been earned.

IN THE THAMES

TWILIGHT IN LYMINGTON RIVER

# CHAPTER II

## THE ISLAND LANDFALL

I YAWNED voluminously as I stood in the well. It was still the twilight of dawn, but I had had to rouse out after all. The sensation of good tide running to waste had been with me—I suppose—even in sleep.

Dover Harbour light and the South Foreland were still flashing in the half-dawn ; the hour was 4 a.m. A grey, chilly morning made Dover cliffs and town look desolate, and a stiff breeze was blowing. At half-past four we made sail and were away, leaving Dover Harbour by the western entrance.

" Cheerless enough," my shipmate growled, as he eyed the seascape outside, a waste of grey, furrowed with wind. I stood at the tiller, juggling it to and fro to keep her on the wind, for the waves that broke on her bow were always throwing her off.

To and fro, shoreward and offshore again, we beat. Shakespeare Cliff, with its chalk face, was left ; and, after the broken slopes of the Warren, Folkestone was near. Off Folkestone the tide turned, and the job of getting on at all, against wind and tide, became decidedly exacting. At times, in lulls between the gusts, we were even set back; we looked along the steamer-pier, with the packet boats alongside, as we headed inshore, and then, on the next board, we had exactly the same view.

This was " as you were " ; no gain at all on that tack.

" I can get that jib in a bit flatter," I said, as I watched my shipmate's jealous efforts, he being now at the tiller. " Shake her for one instant," I added.

The strain in sheeting in the headsails from the well of a yacht falls largely upon the abdominal muscles. But with the wind in the sail one might strain the muscles till they burst. Not a quarter of an inch would be gained. Quite on the contrary, once the sheet was uncleated, out it would run—however manfully one might pull. Hand on sheet, I waited to see the first ghost of a flutter in the jib, and the spray rattled on my face and oilskin. A moment's shaking sufficed ; I gave one mighty hike, and snapped the sheet on the cleat again. " Right-oh," I shouted.

" What's that tramp's game ? " I speculated, as we went about after the next board inshore. A tramp steamer was bound up-Channel, a Portuguese. She steamed close in to Folkestone pier head, slowed speed as if to scrutinize it, and then—without exchange of any signal with the shore—turned sharply off and proceeded to Dover. We chuckled. There had not been much nautical science about her navigation from Dungeness if she had been within an ace of dropping into the wrong port. " Beg pardon ; wrong shop, this," my shipmate commented ; " I meant to go next door."

The clouds were dark to windward ; the lower sky was a smudge of ink by the time that we had passed Hythe, and rain was blurring all the sealine. Then, with a sweep and a whistle, the stronger wind threw itself upon us ; it came all in a moment, of squall strength. The sea was leaping, dirty green ; it was breaking into new foam-caps, and the air was thick with rain. The yacht heeled abruptly, and thrashed heavily as she fought her way on ; then the rain tailed off, and the atmosphere cleared for one moment.

" *There's* Dungeness ! "

Yes, we had raised the lighthouse. The promontory itself, being merely a tongue of flat shingle, was below the horizon. Detached from the land and sticking up solitary as the Eddystone from the sea, there the lighthouse was. Then the stinging rain obscured everything once more.

Folkestone motor luggers were here and there, evidently on their fishing grounds, and they broke sheets of spray from the green seas. With wind and rain, it was dirty weather.

Gradually we made good our way, lurching to and fro, towards the Point ; slow work it was, too, against the tide, and the whole morning went by. Noon had come and gone before we were there.

" There's not the same weight in the puffs," I said ; " the wind is easing."

We loosed the collars of our oilskins, for the deluge was over, and we scanned the sky to windward. That spray had ceased to smother us, and the sky was certainly lightening.

" Look ! "

One of us pointed an eager finger. A thin streak

of colour was upon the sea—it surely meant a glint of sunlight there. It was a herald ; for, all of a sudden, came the wonderful change. The clouds rolled up and parted, sunshine flooded out, and the wind dropped to a breeze.

" Marvellous," my companion said, stripping off his oilskin and kicking it untidily into the cabin. Sea and sky alike had become blue in the space of a few minutes.

It is surprising how swiftly the sun dries up a sodden deck ; patches of the planks, between the long, dark lines of caulking, were already showing the lighter colour of dry wood.

I looked approvingly on the sunlit white of sails and painted coach-roof against the background of blue sea. But I shook my head.

" It's overdone," I grumbled, as (myself at the tiller now) I did my best to weather the extreme tip of Dungeness. " This wind's going to drop entirely, and the tide's on the turn."

Sure enough the wind was falling more and more to a useless whisper, and we rocked and tumbled among blue waves, lifeless. The yellow shingle-bank, with its white buildings and black-banded lighthouse, lay close aboard.

" What's the grouse about it, anyway ? " My companion's tone was serene as he turned back the tips of his jersey sleeves, wet on his wrists in spite of the oilskin. " The new tide will help us." While he spoke, he was spreading things out to dry in the sunlight.

True, the west-going stream—when it gathered—

OFF DUNGENESS

would carry us on our way. But, in the meantime, the anxiety was this. A definite indraught sets into the East Road, and, if we were sucked in, we might contrive to miss the west-going stream rather badly. Two ketches, becalmed to southward of us, were being drawn inshore obviously, by the beam. We were ourselves quite close to the beach, and the waves were breaking. Had I expected this for one moment I would have given the point a berth.

"Wind!" I breathed a sigh of relief as the leech of the mainsail took a pleasant curve again, and the yacht sprang to life. Past the yellow shingle-bank and past the tall lighthouse tower we sailed, and Dungeness dropped astern.

Those ketches, of course, were Rye smacks; and when we opened away from the point they seemed as if they were on the beach, so closely were they skirting the shore up towards Rye.

Fairlight Cliffs in the distance, earth-coloured, glowed with the afternoon sunlight as we gradually raised them. Sailing for pleasure, and not for a fast passage, I like to skirt the shore as much as I reasonably can; the view of the coastline is more than ample compensation for any time lost. Hastings Cliffs, upstanding there and modelled in sun and shadow, were splendid; then came Hastings itself, the old fisher-town between the hills. The whole thing was a panorama.

"The little bright surf-breathing town" of Coventry Patmore's poem, red-roofed in its hollow, is old-world still. And the luggers are hauled up

SUNSET AT BEACHY HEAD

on the beach. But those old Hastings luggers are less old-world than they were, for they seldom seem to set their mainsails now; it is always a matter of motor and mizen. One or two of the bluff, tarry hulls went by us, under power of course. The long sea-fronts of modern Hastings and St. Leonard's were next abeam, and then the low cliffs of Bexhill. So we gradually made good a pleasant passage towards the distant landfall of Beachy Head.

"This is perfect; give me this for ever." My shipmate's tone was steeped in contentment, as, lounging in the cockpit, he carried his eyes from the brown cliffs astern to the distant chalk headland, grey against the sun-glitter on the sea.

But nothing lasts. Before we were off Pevensey (and we crossed the shoal-water of the Royal Sovereign, for the sea, though frisky, was quite harmless), dusk was upon us. Sunset was golden along the west.

"Binnacle and side-lights now," I muttered dutifully, and I surrendered the tiller. And, as the yacht thrashed and tumbled in the busy sea-way, I crept through into the fo'c'sle, where the thump of the hitting waves outside always sets up such a noise. The coloured lights were soon fixed in their brackets. Foam that creamed away on either side was white no longer—it was a shimmer of silver grey; with one arm threaded through the shrouds, I stood and watched it for a while when my job was done. There is a fascination in that streaming furrow.

Night had soon settled on the seascape. Beachy Head was close aboard of us, and the lighthouse sent its wheeling beam round, first casting a spot of light on the white cliffs behind it, and then throwing it (as a fisherman might cast a fly) sixteen miles to sea. The town-lamps of Eastbourne, a bright galaxy of white and yellow stars all a-twinkle, were falling astern, and the mass of Beachy was huge in the night. It towered—a black mountain —beside us. The cliff, as we rounded it, jutted farther and farther astern of us, and its dark bulk expunged the sparkle of Eastbourne, light by light.

" Look at the lights going out ! *Flick, flick, flick,*" I said.

*Flick, flick, flick,* they were snapped into darkness as the cliff came between, till, with a final *flick*, the last light went out. We were alone in the darkness, and tumbling in the overfalls.

The breeze now blowing was stiff, and we passed rapidly by the Seven Sisters—seen only as a dark loom of land in the night. Then the lights of Seaford began to twinkle, almost in one with those of Newhaven. Merrily we bowled on.

" That's Newhaven," I said, " and it's not midnight yet ; we aren't doing too badly."

" Where's the Breakwater light ? " My companion was sceptical about it. The light certainly looked a puny effort, hardly to be identified. But at this very moment a steamer emerged from behind it, shaping course seaward. There was no doubt of the place.

" Then, seeing it's bed-time, why not go into the harbour, and make ourselves at home ? "

" Honest ? " I asked.

He chuckled—a chuckle of absolute contentment. " Not for worlds," he said.

We could have a short sleep in turn ; and neither of us wanted more. We were happier out here in the summer night.

There was quite a sprinkle of small lights on the sea just here.

"Those mast-head lights are trawlers, of course," I said; "but there are others—are *they* boats?" In point of fact, they proved to be lighted buoys to mark the nets. They all dropped astern, and the dark sea was again unbroken.

The wind fell lighter during the night, and, when the tide had again turned against us, progress became much less satisfying.

"Have you put Brighton astern yet?" was my companion's first question when, after a brief nap, he emerged from the cabin doorway into the starlight. Brighton lights were brilliant on the horizon, but I could not bring them nearer; they hung there. And the dark hours went by.

Starlight overhead remained unclouded, and at last a faint sensation of dawn was felt. It was only a hint, a shadowy lightening of tone. Almost too vague to be perceived, it stole somehow into the scheme of things. Yes, the binnacle would soon be extinguished now; here was another day. We leaned in the well, and the sails above us began to be a dull grey, black no longer.

"D'you get the scent?" I asked suddenly, as I peered over the sea that was grey in the dawn. We were some miles offshore, yet from somewhere a strong smell of hay came to our nostrils. It came for one moment over the water, and was gone. This is a curious and freakish way that smells sometimes have—this of carrying for miles over the sea. I remember a day when, some miles offshore,

I was watching a mass of thundercloud from which
a storm was breaking over the land. Suddenly,
across those miles of sea, came the unmistakable
smell of rain-laid dust.

" Brighton is fairly abeam now," I said, looking
at the line of lights. The time was half-past four,
and the breeze had quickened a trifle ; the coast
lay dark and blurred in the dawn, and the daybreak
looked none too settled. From Brighton we laid
course for Worthing, and the line of shore fell away
from us again. But, against the tide, progress was
slow work.

" There's the sun ! " A red ball, it glowed
astern of us, and here was full day again. Binnacle
was extinguished and side-lights stowed.

Worthing had been left astern by seven o'clock,
and my shipmate went below to get breakfast.
The yacht was vigorous enough now, for the wind
had breezed up with conviction. When she went
a little off the wind, she brought her chine right
out, and, when luffed, she was inclined to run into
the wind too quickly. She wanted a world of
humouring, and was clearly over-canvassed. So, as
the sky was clouding, and the wind seemed stiff-
ening more and more every moment, I decided to
pull a reef down. It was a really hard breeze now.

" Lend a hand," I shouted below ; " we'll have
to reef."

" And the tea just made," came the aggrieved
reply.

Now here had arisen the ideal conditions in which
a small barge yacht can show herself troublesome.

She will not easily lie to ; she wants a hand on the helm, or she will run into mischief at once. The spritsail barge has no need to reef ; she brails her mainsail, or, if necessary, strikes her topsail—and neither operation occupies a tithe of the time needed for reefing. If we could have hove to we could have breakfasted before reefing. As it was, we would get the job done at once, although it spoiled our breakfast.

Reefed now, we drew seaward again on a long leg, with the spray flying. But the skies were again blue, with rolling white cloud only, and the foam was dazzling white also. This was a glorious morning ; the sea was alive.

We missed Littlehampton on the long board seaward—the familiar little harbour and town were away on the skyline—but we sailed close inshore at Bognor ; and, at the Shelley Rocks buoy, I came to a decision. I had been thinking hard.

" We've got to mend our pace if we're going to save our tide through the tide-race in the Looe. It's useless attempting it, on a wind, unless the tide will take us through."

The wind had steadied a little since the return of the sunshine ; so we took the risk and shook out the reef. With foam streaking away from us, we were soon slashing down in great style past the shingly shore and flat landscape of Selsey Bill, headed for the Mixon Beacon. If we missed our tide we should have to sail right round the Owers, seven miles offshore. I watched the clock. Yes, she could do it.

" See the overfalls—waiting for us on the other side."

The Bill, and the shoal-system seaward of it, was sheltering us considerably at present, and the sea was not rough in the Looe. But the overfalls were a different matter—a regular system of shoal-breakers, a turmoil of foam.

" We'll get a dusting ! " I grinned, with a cheerfulness that was partly simulated ; for, like most other people, I hate a tide-race.

The Mixon Beacon was astern ; we were there.

*Thud !* Into the first wave *Growler* drove, and we were drenched in spray ; but the first wave had killed her speed. If I had luffed more I should have kept her drier. Almost a-shake, she was quite manageable ; one could gauge progress by the buoys—the tide was taking her through.

But it was a curious progress, as such progress in a tide-race always is. The waves simply *pounded* on her, and the lift and tumble were steep and very sudden. The waves beat on her hollow hull like on a drum.

" Ever hear such a row ? " my companion chirped, as an extra big one hit its solid blow. " Bang ! "

The passage through the overfalls was brief, and, from a steadier well now, we were able to take pleasant stock of the landfall which had first opened at Selsey Bill. Twelve miles distant, the cliff reared itself nobly in the sunlight—the white face of Culver. There lay the Isle of Wight.

There it lay. We had rounded our last headland, and had reached the Waters of the Wight. It was only a minor nuisance that the wind took off to such an extent that we were persistently swept by the tide to leeward of our true course for Bembridge. This meant patient work to windward on a lee-going tide ; but as soon as we had closed the shore, and were out of the full run of the tidal stream, we were able to make it good. Not that the delay was of any real consequence. We were able to reach the Drumhead buoy by the time that there was sufficient water to enter. Before eight o'clock that evening, *Growler* had crept up the narrow tideway, and was comfortably moored in Bembridge Harbour. We looked about us with contented eyes as we tied the gaskets on the mainsail. Before ten we had turned in, and were deep in that comfortable sleep which follows when a passage, however small, is a thing accomplished.

# CHAPTER III

## WATERS OF THE WIGHT

THE fitting approach to the Waters of the Wight is from the open sea. And here we were. This whole system of landlocked sea was ours to explore—this pleasant hunting-ground of creek and estuary.

Though *Growler* was a stranger here, I myself was not ; I knew these waters pretty well already. She, too, would now make her pilgrimage among them, and—east-coaster in every line of her—she would feel a sense of home in many a creek which is cousin of her own anchorages about the Blackwater or Thames.

From Chichester to Poole this system of waters extends ; and the Island itself—a bulwark of weather-shore—is in the middle. The first glimpse of that fairy Island—caught, as we caught it, off Selsey Bill—had been a thing of beauty ; but perhaps the really ideal landfall is at the other end —the Needles.

To all of us who cruise hereabout, or who sail up-Channel to the Wight, the approach to the Needles is familiar ; and the impression never fails of its magic. Over blue seas, the great cliffs are white and gracious ; through the flying squall they loom in majesty. And, either way, they are unforgettable.

Let me recall a passage ; and also I want to say a few words on the subject in general, before we continue our regular exploration. We had raised the Island several hours ago, and there it now towered, its white cliffs abrupt, above the seaway. Waves were breaking to spindrift round the Needles.

The fairway buoys, that mark the regular deep-water entrance to the Needles Channel, are west of the Needles Rocks ; we could see the buoys tossing in the welter of green and white. I had neglected them of set purpose, and the yacht's bowsprit was pointed at the Island. A long line of foam, a smother of white, lay between ; it was right over the bows.

" *Shoal !* " my companion called, and he jerked his arm to point it ; the gesture was eloquent.

But I held my course ; I had seen this before. The waves as they broke looked ugly enough—just as if they were thrashing on a shoal with only a foot or so over it. And the wind was boisterous.

But this was only the tide-rip, as I told him, while I juggled the tiller this way and that. The tide in the Needles Channel runs at five knots or more, while in Christchurch Bay the current is comparatively slow. Along the edge, between the two tides, runs that rip of breaking sea. It looked formidable, but—beyond throwing a little more spray about our oilskins—it would do us no manner of harm. The wind whistled, the low clouds scudded, and the yacht drove on.

Everywhere were crests of foam, not only in the tide-rip (which was a regular welter), but in the

NEARING THE NEEDLES

fairway too. And through the noise and tumult we steered for the Solent—itself a busy seaway to-day. This was a squall-wind, and was getting ragged already. Up the Solent *Growler* scudded. At Jack-in-the-Basket her course was changed abruptly, and she was immediately between the long, tidal flats of Lymington River, in complete shelter. We reached up the river, with that singular sense of comfort and smoothness which is felt at its best only after a rough passage. A mooring was found ; we furled the sails. One more day's work was done.

.    .    .    .    .

Loitering on board, in the dusk of that same day, it came to me (as more than once before) that the place offered a summary of the whole Solent region. Here were the tidal reaches and flat banks about us, and there, opposite, was the great bulwark—the Island, which shelters this system of quiet waters from the Channel storms.

I made some such remark to my shipmate. The two of us were busy in the well of the yacht, washing up the supper things, and the clean crockery stood about us. Just a moment ago one strong gleam of level sunlight had broken through ; it had shone, tawny-gold, across the brown rushes of the tidal flat, and had set the distant Isle of Wight aglow. From between clouds this had been a final glitter, and the sun had set.

I made my remark, but my companion looked at me, blank-faced. His whole mind was absorbed with the coffee-jug which he was drying. Then he spoke.

"Let's get the crockery below," he said; and I came into line. Perhaps I wore a grin of forbearance as I settled the plates in the racks and hung up the cups. Seeing that I happen to be owner and skipper of the yacht, it speaks volumes for my democratic principles that I allow myself to be put in my place like that.

Meanwhile, the tide brimmed up, and the wind had fallen to an air, so that the water was almost mirror-like. Together we put our chins on our hands and looked out towards the Island.

"More like a Scotch loch than the Solent. The Island in this dusk is just like mountains."

Our work finished, my companion felt free to admit the existence of landscape; he was filling his pipe as he spoke.

We sat on the cabin-top and idled. There is no place on earth where the perfection of idleness can be realised so thoroughly as on a yacht at anchor; the sense is at its highest in a quiet creek after a bit of a dusting outside. Our sails were stowed, ropes coiled, cabin tidied. There was no task undone to trouble the conscience. And we idled. We just sat in the twilight.

There is a feeling, a quality, about these tidal fringes that quite eludes the telling. These waters need to be discovered; they possess an atmosphere of their own which may not be at once felt by the casual comer. Missing a certain angle of vision, the chance comer is apt to miss the real thing. The

inspiration is subtle, and it is not always caught in
a moment.

Silence and remoteness were entire to-night.
The last packet boat from the Isle of Wight had
gone by us ; the excursion steamers from Bournemouth, with their splash-splashing paddle-wheels,
were no doubt homeward bound somewhere, their
decks crowded. Ashore, at this very moment, the
roads would still be noisy with motor-cars, on the
Island not less than the mainland. Passengers
afloat or ashore would be getting their own glimpses
of the Waters of the Wight in their own way. But
they were passengers only. For us this water region
was a place of abode. With all its rivers and creeks
that spread—tentacle fashion—into the solid land,
it lay about us here.

The Isle of Wight, set clear of the mainland,
and screening from the southerly gales a navigable
stretch of water, was a gift of Nature to the south
coast of England. No awkward river-bar or tortuous
entrance hindered the approach ; the old shipmaster could seek the gradual shelter of the island,
and bring up securely under its lee. St. Helens
Roads, Cowes Roads, Yarmouth Roads were among
the open anchorages which he could use. But
Nature had gone farther yet. She had not only
provided roadsteads, but had linked up with this
landlocked strait a series of natural harbours,
naturally sheltered. Obvious sites alike for ports
and for shipyards were thus provided—from Poole
to Chichester they range. The approaches to
Poole are sheltered by the rocky Isle of Purbeck ;

the entrances to Southampton, Portsmouth, Langston, and Chichester lie under the lee of the Isle of Wight.    And the smaller inlets on both sides of the strait were not less valued ; they were places of account when shipping was still small : Lymington, Yarmouth, Newtown, Brading, and so on—each one of them has given harbourage to some of the proudest shipping of earlier days.

The reaches of water or of marsh inlets are a level foreground to distant downs, downs that are dark and solid under the white cumulus.    These are the hills that give the shelter.    The hills are abrupt on their southward face, with cliffs to the sea.  But they are quiet and gradual on the side which faces the inlets.    Freshwater Down has its sheer fall of chalk cliff, from 400 feet high, to the English Channel.    But, from this side, we see only the gradual slopes.    Purbeck is iron-bound seaward, but Poole Harbour sees only the gentle contours.

Home is the sailor, home from the sea.

That really is the sensation which these waters convey, and it is felt more than usual on an evening like this.

I looked across at my companion, silent in the half-light.    He sat up and knocked the ashes out of his pipe.

" Almost always high water," he said, and yawned.    " It'll stay like this for hours yet."

On other coasts the tide rises steadily to high water, and then drops by gradual stages to low.

But here we have the double high tide : two high waters and one low.

This disproportionate amount of high water, a curious effect, is brought about—in a rather complex fashion—by interplay of the tidal streams which, divided by one end of the Island, come together at the other end of it. There are various minor effects, as, for instance, the considerable difference between the rise and fall of tide at opposite ends of the Solent. But everything works with calculable regularity.

That being so, it is rather odd to find that Drayton, who knew perfectly well that the double tides run like clockwork, should have seen fit to name them among " those prodigious signes . . . which the Britans wrack fore-ran " :

> The Seas against their course with double Tides returne,
> And oft were seene by night like boyling pitch to burne.

But Drayton has other things as well to say respecting the tides ; he had a very good appreciation of them. Speaking of the Isle of Wight, he went on to say :

> And to the Northe, betwixt the fore-land and the firme,
> She hath that narrow Sea, which we the *Solent* tearme :
> Where those rough irefull Tides, as in her Straits they meet,
> With boysterous shocks and rores each other rudely greet.
> Which fierclie when they charge, and sadlie make retreat,
> Upon the bulwarkt Forts of *Hurst* and *Calsheot* beat.

From both points of view, the tides are an object of importance to the explorer of the Solent. The

SUNSET AT LYMINGTON

double high water will often be found quite an amenity in the creeks, and the strength of the tides themselves in the Solent, those "rough irefull Tides," will soon exact respect outside. Only with a commanding breeze has the small-boat sailor a chance of making good against the tide in its strength through the Needles Channel, when it runs at five and a half knots; but the tides, formidable as an enemy, can be turned into an equally powerful friend. To work one's tides is essential. And the small-boat sailor will find that he should work from west to east when exploring the inlets of the Solent, and not vice versa. The reason is simple. His favouring tide from the westward will give him the flowing stream up the creek or harbour in which he intends to anchor. The tide that brings him from the eastward, on the other hand, will carry him to the mouth of his creek when the ebb is pouring seaward from it. Save in a commanding breeze, he will probably have to let go his anchor and wait.

With favouring tide I have entered these creeks and rivers times almost beyond number now. Into Beaulieu, after battling her way up the Solent, through the driven spray, the yacht has slipped quietly, to lose herself (so to speak) in the New Forest. Entering Bembridge, I have brought up with the Isle of Wight downs for near neighbour. Or here at Lymington I have entered at dusk, when the wind has gone and the tide alone has brought the yacht in. You can listen on such evenings to the talking of the town through the twilight. Silent as the yacht herself, I have been able to hear the noise of the children playing and of the dogs barking long before I have reached my anchorage. The church clock has chimed from somewhere beyond. There has been no other sound as the yacht drifted ghost-like up the river.

Also, when one roams ashore for some twilight

stroll the serenity is no less. Just when the high
water is brimming up beside the grassy sea-walls I
have paced in the dusk that is cool after a day of
rain. Or I have wandered on the lonely gorse-
covered reaches or have paced the sand-levels at low
water, watching the great continents of rolling
cloud over the uplands. Mere enumeration is idle;
but these things it is that form the background of
the Waters of the Wight. ·

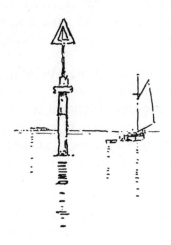

# CHAPTER IV

## IDLE HOURS AT BEMBRIDGE

A WEEK or two had elapsed before we next came to Bembridge. Bembridge entrance, being tidal, is not a place always open ; and, after a passage delayed by foul winds, we managed to arrive when the Drumhead buoy was high and dry and the rocks were uncovered to shoreward of it. Not being a crab, the yacht could not enter. So overboard went the anchor with a splash. We had missed the tide ; and there was nothing for it but to wait.

A brisk westerly wind was blowing, so that the shelter of that ancient weather-shore of St. Helens was welcome enough during the hour or two of patience. Like most other sailing men I abhor tumbling about in an exposed anchorage, or, alternatively, standing off and on, over and over again, in order to kill time. We are all alike in loving to sail the whole clock round when we do it for choice, and in hating to sail a single hour when we don't do it of our own free will. The weather-shore was acceptable, and we waited in the sunlight. The sun was broad over the Island, making toward the west.

Nothing really comes amiss, and nothing could have been more pleasurable than this little interlude. Taking advantage of the barge hull, we had worked so close inshore before anchoring that the sandy bottom was clear in perfect detail below us, with small patches of seaweed and small stones upon it— seen through limpid water. No longer at sea, we were in the shallows ; we were almost aground on the Island.

Meanwhile, we could look into the harbour, where yachts were afloat in that small basin of deeper water which we could not reach. Then we watched the tide begin to cover the rocks and to creep by slow degrees higher on the bar.

" Might have a shot now," I said, after a long interval. " It doesn't matter a rap if we do take the sand. The tide will float us off almost at once."

The yacht slowly approached the buoy, leaving the stone-built fort on St. Helens Sand to seaward of her. The sun had set, and the group flashing light on the fort glittered every ten seconds. The fairway light also shone, a red star, in the harbour.

The sandbank separating the tideway from the sea was still bare and dry, and the tide gurgled past the steep edge of sand in a little torrent, carrying us in.

" Look at it racing—it bubbles like a brook after a thunderstorm. See it lick, lick, lick, higher on the sand."

The tide sent us in, past the ferry (deserted in the twilight), and we manœuvred carefully through the press of moored yachts. Some management was wanted.

" If it's a clear place, look out for it—sure to be shallow, or they'd have put a mooring there."

But finally *Growler* was herself tied up to a mooring. The wind had fallen to nothing with the
sunset ; and the tide, as it brimmed higher and
higher in the late dusk, made the harbour a level
lake.

" Perfectly landlocked," my companion commented, as we lingered, after furling the sails. The
last gasket on the mainsail had just been tied.

" A strong north-easter can stir things up a bit
at high water," I said. " But it's very snug."

The calm was perfect ; the reflections of masts
and hulls scarcely wavered, and last twilight faded
into night.

.        .        .        .        .

Morning that followed was to bring no new
adventure and no fresh exploration for the present.
I merely set the sails to the idle sunlight just to dry
them thoroughly, and then coated the mainsail and
stowed the headsails in the locker. The yacht was
to stay in port for a time. Here she lay in the
landlocked lake—a peaceful contrast to the tumbling
seaways which we had left. Swans were afloat on
the blue water here.

For a few days of sunshine I remained there,
living on board. These periods in harbour are not
to be despised. I roamed over the downs and along
the shore-side day by day. Then the crisp little
breeze which had come to ripple the harbour each
morning fell away to nothing, leaving a motionless
calm, the water smooth like oil.

" I don't care for the look of it," I thought ;

SOUTHWARD ALONG THE SHORE FROM BEMBRIDGE

" this is the end of the fine weather. Not, of course, that it matters a pin, being in harbour." But I went to look at the glass, and it told clearly of mischief in store.

Sure enough that night the wind came down in a torrent of strength and noise. From the downs and between the shores it " funnels " through the harbour. All night it was rampant, and every noise that an anchored ship can conjure was busy about me. The mooring-chain, the lee-boards, the rudder, the rigging—each of them was doing its clank, or grind, or whine ; and the wind whooped and shouted, while the water washed, washed, washed, as we rocked to the storm. Then the rain came with a rush. It found one or two spots in the caulking which the sun had opened—one of them above my own unfortunate head as I lay. The night was a night of noise and fury ; but the weather-shore was close aboard, and I turned over and forgot it all in sleep.

Perfect though the shelter was, a small dinghy might easily get itself swamped while being pulled ashore in this weather. During the day or two that followed care was needed as I struggled at the oars to prevent too much water being shipped. That wind blew for a couple of days, and then abated in torrents of rain. And, after rain, there was a strange allurement in the wet twilight when, ashore alone for a spell, I paced sometimes over the rough tracks, looking landward, across the marsh-land that was once tidal salting, towards the grey downs beyond.

BEMBRIDGE DOWN

That broad level, joined as it formerly was to the present inlet, was all a part of Brading Harbour. It is said that, as late as the reign of Charles II, the harbour extended to Brading High Street, and that ships used to anchor beside the old houses there. A regular expanse of inland water existed when the Danes entered in 896 and King Alfred's ships surprised them. Brading, with its harbour, grew to considerable importance in the centuries that followed; and Sir John Oglander described it, in the reign of Charles I, as " formerly ye only towne for receypt of strangors that came by shippinge." " Ride and Cows," he said, were " no then knowen," whereas Brading was (by his account) " ye awntientest towne in owre Island." As a port it once contained Ryde, Sandown, and Shanklin in its boundaries.

In a grim twilight I pulled back on board to-night, and the day which followed was grey and grim. The harbour, apart from the basin which has been dredged, is very shallow, and the whole of the centre is a mud flat. My present mooring, above the boat-houses, gave only a couple of feet of water at low tide. The lake dwindles at the ebb, and in the middle of the harbour that broad mud island appears—a little drear to some eyes, perhaps, in days of wind and rain, but never less than congenial to me. The tide-forsaken flats possess their own charm, and I have no personal prejudice in favour of high water.

Once or twice, in those days of storm-wind, I had ranged afoot over the flat sand toward St. Helens

AT BEMBRIDGE

IN COWES WEEK—FLAT CALM

Fort at low tide, with the water on both sides and the wind roaring. To-day I went ashore at St. Helens.

The wind was again blowing great guns from the south-west, but—under the little cliff of St. Helens —one could lose it entirely, and out on Spithead itself was no sea at all which could inconvenience a ship of even moderate tonnage when lying at anchor. The St. Helens anchorage was high in favour in old days, not only because of its shelter, but because, from it, the fleet could get to sea at once, blow the wind from what quarter it might. The Needles Passage, not having then been properly surveyed, was never used by the fleet in earlier days.

It is interesting, as one stands on the St. Helens shore, to recall some of its many associations. In 1545, Henry VIII's fleet was anchored here at St. Helens. The French approached it in superior force, and the royal ships retreated into the narrows of Spithead, hoping to lure the Frenchmen on to the shoals. But the enemy were too wary to rise to the bait, and they diverted their attack elsewhere. In point of fact, they landed an invading force on the Island.

In 1690 Torrington was lying here when word was brought that Tourville had beeen sighted off St. Albans Head ; the fleet put to sea, and battle was joined off Beachy Head. In 1740 Anson's *Centurion* sailed from the same anchorage for her famous voyage round the world, returning to Portsmouth four years later laden with fabulous

wealth. In 1778 H.M.S. *Victory*, then a new
100-gun ship (Admiral Keppel), set sail against the
French at Brest under d'Orvilliers ; and that same
H.M.S. *Victory* (dry-docked at Portsmouth) is not
many miles from St. Helens now.

The virtue of St. Helens did not consist in its
weather-shore alone, great as that boon was. It had
another. St. Helens possessed a spring of water of
wonderful " keeping " quality, which was much
in request for the filling of the water-casks of
ships outward bound. From the sixteenth to the
eighteenth century, the whole fleet was accustomed
to water here for that very reason.

St. Helens itself had been a port possessing fifty
ships of its own, and " twenty good shipmasters " ;
it declined gradually as Cowes—in the eighteenth
century—began to develop.

I scrambled up the cliff to the seamark, which
looks like a painted board from seaward, but is at
once seen—from the landward side—to be a real
church tower. Built in the thirteenth century, it
was abandoned in 1717 in favour of a newer church
inland, and it fell to ruin, all except its tower,
which, strengthened with new brickwork, was
retained as a seamark.

Back on board in the evening, I watched a glimpse
of sunlight sweep seaward in the driving rack. In
hope of a clearing, I lingered to watch the dusk and
the leaden landscape ; but no other gleam followed,
and the night closed in with driving rain.

.    .    .    .    .

A FRIGATE UNDER FULL SAIL

But ill weather cannot last for ever, and, when we were next away for some minor expedition, the wind—no longer violent—had fallen to the other extreme. Such light air as stirred was barely enough to ruffle the water, and the sun shone. We were soon out of the cabin. The tide was at about half ebb, and we made sail immediately.

"Humph! we've cut things a trifle fine," I said. "It may be a little awkward."

A light puff of westerly breeze sent us down to the ferry; but then—under the combined effect of failing wind and of weather-shore—we found ourselves becalmed and out of control. It was essential that, if we were to make good our escape, we should remain faithful to the channel, steering, between the buoys, to the Drumhead. But the ebb-tide sets right away seaward over St. Helens Sand, and it was setting us, beamwise, out of the channel right over the sandbank. If we touched we should, of course, stay there. The white buoys, moreover, were useless as guides, for, sagging over the flat to the full extent of their cables, they were only just afloat in the very shallowest of water. Sagging eastward like them, as we were, we should soon be aground for the day. I jumped to seize the long boat-hook, using it as a quant-pole to keep us off the flat. Labour was exhausting in this windless sunshine.

"Makes you sweat," my companion grinned, without a particle of sympathy, as he watched my shiny face grow shinier every moment.

"Sweat's dropping off me in streams," I panted. "But I don't want to provide a free spectacle for Bembridge—the ship that didn't! Nor," I added, "do I want to waste a day on St. Helens Sand."

At last the iron shoe of the boat-hook began to strike the shingle of the bar instead of the sand of the flats; we were in sight of freedom. With a breeze that was barely perceptible we drifted past Seaview Pier, mirrored in the calm blue water. Bembridge lay in the sunlight astern, successfully left. The sea had left it too; it was shut off from the sea by nearly a mile of sand.

# CHAPTER V

## TO COWES IN COWES WEEK

OUR next departure from Bembridge stood in complete contrast. I was intending to shift round to Cowes for Cowes Week, and conditions—on the night before—seemed ideal. The wind, which was then south-westerly, had been so for days. It promised, therefore, to give us a comfortable reach round under the lee of the Island in the morning. An early start would be needed so that we should get the west-going stream in Spithead.

"If we get away at seven, it will do," I had decided overnight. "Even if the wind is light, we shall push out somehow. Of course, the wind *may* play us a low trick. If it veers northerly at all it will bottle us here in the harbour till the turn of the tide. But there ought to be no chance of that ; the glass has no tendency to rise." And so we turned in.

I was out on deck at six in the morning, and I snorted with indignation. The sunshine was delightful, but the wind was blowing hard from the north-west. Sweeping round St. Helens cliff into the harbour, it was dead foul.

"Tumble up !" I shouted below. "A foul wind. And it's strong ; we must pull a reef down."

My companion, now in the well, made a very wry

53

mouth as he looked about him. Wind and tide would do all they could to keep us from the Drumhead. " What about it ? " he said.

" We'll have a shot, but I hae ma doots," I replied as I tied the reef points. " And, if we can't make the Drumhead against the flood, we've missed the tide outside."

We would do our best, and see. The yacht heeled away from the breeze, and reached across in splendid style to the ferry. Down went the helm, and she essayed to turn to windward against the tide in that very narrow fairway.

A small racing yacht would have made nothing of the business, but a barge was at her worst, and powerless. Try as she would, she simply could not manage to escape ; there was really no room for a yacht of her size to gather way and so to stand a fair chance. To and fro she went, seeking to zig-zag to freedom, but the tide sucked her back every time, by the beam. It was no good.

" Let go ! "

So we let go our anchor with that familiar clatter of running chain, somewhere opposite the Club-house, there to await the deepening of the water over the banks ; we could then reach out, clean over the St. Helens Sand, not bothering about the fairway at all. But I knew that we had lost our tide to Cowes. One's fancy overnight had seen us berthed snugly in Cowes River by half-past ten this August morning, but half-past nine found us in fact still at Bembridge, just making sail for our second effort. The sands had been covered within an hour or two, and a great sheet of blue water, broken into little waves, stretched to eastward of us. The anchor was hove in short and broken out. Over the sand flew the yacht with a few inches of water under her lee-board ; the tide, of course, was rising and a touch could not have mattered a bit, but I breathed more freely all the same when we had cleared the sand. It was good to be at sea again. With any sort of luck, it might still be possible to make Cowes before half-past one, the hour at which the Solent stream would turn against us ; true, the river tide would be ebbing, but no matter ; the wind would be fair for the entrance.

Out in Spithead, with wind against tide, the usual steep sea was running, and we were deluged with spray. The yacht banged and thumped among the breaking hillocks of water, making a vast noise and turmoil of it. Those are the things that knock all the speed out of a boat—those vicious breaking foam-caps that *hit* her—hit, hit, hit her. Despite the tide under us, we seemed to creep ; progress was wretchedly slow ; we had weathered Ryde, it was true, but we had only just brought Wootton Creek abeam when the tide had turned, and we were still several miles from Cowes. The earliest sign of changing tide is the set of the current inshore, which begins to run easterly some time before the turn of the tidal stream itself—the " Cowes Tide " they call it locally. A yacht anchored close to the land had swung to face the altered current long before the tide had turned out here in the open fairway.

When the tide did turn, progress—slow already —became more poor than ever. Every patient board gained incredibly little ; but still we worked on, and at half-past four in the afternoon (not half-past ten in the morning !) we had won our way to Old Castle Point, and were drawing level with the

OLD CASTLE POINT AND WEST COWES.

bevy of crowded vessels which forested the road-stead with masts. The royal yacht at her moorings was close abeam.

But we were not into Cowes yet. So near and yet so far. That sluicing tide round the Point was too much for us ; weather that corner we could not. We tried hard, tried and tried again, but it was no use, and down went the anchor. We had gained sight of Cowes and were in some shelter, but

that was all.  I was anxious to be at my berth
before night ;  otherwise we should have sat there
awaiting the tide with our customary patience.  As
it was, I was glad for once of a tow.

We finished our passage securely, but in complete
ignominy.  A Cowes smack, under motor power,
came from the eastward within an hour, and her
we hailed.

" Give us a pluck into the river ? "

Now Cowes folk make no pretence of general
altruism during Cowes Week ;  the world is with
them for a week only in the year, and they exact
the uttermost—even from the most obscure hanger-
on of the great occasion.  The answer was obvious.

" What' you goin' to give us if we do ? "

The boat slowed her engine as she circled round
us ;  and I asked them what they wanted.

" Oh, we shan't charge you much ;  we'll do
it very moderate.  A couple of quid'll do it for
you."

I had expected as much ;  but my reply—a brief
injunction to " talk sense "—brought a reduced
offer.  " Say a quid, then," they shouted, and their
tone was one of aggrieved generosity.

But I knew that the smack was going into Cowes
in any case and was not likely to leave the price of
several drinks and some tobacco behind her.  So I
shrugged my shoulders and said that I was staying
where I was.

" What *will* you give, then ? " came the inquiry,
now with a strong rasp and asperity about it.

Unashamed, I mentioned the sum of ten shillings,

and the response was immediate. " Chuck us y'r rope over," they said. And thus, at tail of a grubby smack, we arrived among the rank and fashion of Cowes Week.

The strong north wind had cleared the roadstead of all really small craft. Cowes had become a lee shore for the time being, and the anchorage would have been a welter of horrible discomfort for small vessels. They had run for shelter elsewhere, many of them into the Medina. And they were wise, for nothing is more wretched than an uneasy berth.

But Cowes, of course, is no natural anchorage for small yachts, and in the normal course they gravitate elsewhere. Where, inside the river, the shelter is good, the fairway is narrow, and the tides very strong; while, outside, the sea develops something of a lop on the smallest provocation. The roadstead was—and is—snug enough for larger vessels. Cowes, in 1808 is thus mentioned :

" The Town enjoys a good Trade for the Sale of Provisions, especially in time of War, when large Fleets of Merchant Ships often ride here for several Weeks, waiting either for Wind or Convoy."

In 1781 Sir Richard Worsley wrote of it to much the same effect :

" The harbour of Cowes is as safe as any in the British Channel, and by far the most convenient for vessels bound to Holland or the east countries ; it is therefore much frequented by ships, to repair damages sustained at sea, and to winter in, until the season permits them to proceed on their respective voyages."

But things have changed now, and the traffic goes by.  Even in going by, however, it has made itself felt.  The Admiralty directions in the *Channel Pilot* contain a warning to masters of passing steam-ships :

" As considerable damage is caused to boats, wharves, embankments, etc., at Cowes, as well as danger to life, by sudden waves propagated from vessels proceeding at a high rate of speed past the entrance to the harbour, vessels should proceed at a moderate speed when passing through the area."

The same trouble, and even " danger to life " referred to in the directions, has at times befallen the holiday-makers on Southsea beach when, on a fine day, they set up their deck-chairs, or lie on the sand, only a yard or two from the edge of the sea. It is quite calm and no waves breaking.  The wash of a liner can, in these conditions, send ashore a breaking sea like a tidal wave.  Such waves have been known not only to drench the holiday-makers to the skin, but the backwash has sucked them out seawards with it—to the great peril of their lives.

Here, then, we were at Cowes in Cowes Week. We had entered a different atmosphere—an alien atmosphere, one might almost say.  For the casual wanderings which elsewhere are one's happiness have little contact in general with this world here present. One's delight has always been to seek the lonely seaways and sequestered creeks, and to wander self-dependent and detached. Here was the great world, crowded, opulent, and self-conscious.

My hands, battered somewhat from a week's manual labours, became an object of concern—to be doctored drastically with soap and Vim and hot water. I achieved a degree of respectability—at all events to the extent of putting on white bags which were meticulously clean and a yachting cap that was really " snowy-crowned." So equipped, I made my brief digression into the civilised world. A delightful digression it always is. Days spent in racing, during successive Cowes Weeks, as guest of the owners of *White Heather*, *Shamrock*, *Westward*, and many other famous yachts, have always been golden occasions.

Cowes, too, at regatta time, is a memorable sight, especially on the Friday, when every ship is dressed, and the whole of the Road is alive with bunting. In this gay city afloat, one joins some racing yacht. Sail is made. Over the line at sound of the gun the yacht flies—her lee-rail down, and the green water pouring along her scuppers at a riot of speed. She is away for the quietude of the open Solent, greyhound swift, neck and neck, as it were, with some fleet and sunlit rival. Back again, through Cowes Roadstead, as she rounds her course, she returns ; delicately handled, she swerves and doubles and recovers through that congestion of ships—all among the white hulls and the glitter of brasswork and the flutter of bunting. The thing, on a brilliant day, is a regular passage from dreamland.

In the club-houses and along the crowded water-front we who think in terms of sail forgather, and talk the chances of the past day all over again.   From the Fountain to the Signal Station of the R.Y.S. familiar faces are everywhere till late in the evening.

Then perhaps with the most perfect naturalness one steps one morning right out of Cowes Week and into the quiet backwater life of the creeks and inlets.   It was on a day during this particular Cowes Week that, having no race, I elected to wander up to Newport in the sailing dinghy.

The teeming waterside of Cowes, with its ship-yards and moorings, is left at once, and a peaceful inland waterway is opened.   The River Medina above Cowes is still quite primitive and untouched —much, indeed, as it must have looked when Henry VIII built the two defensive castles at the mouth of it.   Leland refers to them thus :

" That set up on the east side of the haven is called the East Cow, and that set up on the west side is called the West Cow, and is the bigger castle of the two."

They were in fact :

> The Two great Cows that in loud thunder roar,
> This on the eastern, that the western shore,
> Where Newport enters stately Wight.

The " great Cow " on the western shore has finally become the Club-house of the Royal Yacht Squadron, and its " loud thunder " is nothing but the modest bang of the gun for the races.

To-day I had left it all. The tide was with me, and, between the green banks, I worked my way, on the wind. A curve of the river opened Newport, a distant town clustered round a church tower; the next turn hid it; then, when opened again, it was much nearer, and the broad river was beginning to narrow. A region of smoke surrounds the chimneys of the Medina Mills, but that is soon passed, and then comes Newport itself, the capital of the Island.

Safely in the centre of the Island, yet approached by a tidal river, the site of Newport was an inevitable one for an early settlement. It dates back to Roman times, and coins of Hadrian and Nero have been found there. The town has seen all the successive changes of garb and face that some eighteen centuries have brought. It still retains something of its old-world air; but it is largely modern, and certainly it is better-conditioned than in the early fifteen-hundreds, of which Sir John Oglander wrote : "In those tymes the stretes weare not paved, but lay most wet and beastlye with great stoppels to stepp over ye Kennell from ye one syde to ye other."

I had reached Newport before the first high water. There was time to get to Carisbrooke and back before the second ebb would leave my dinghy grounded in the mud and so prevent my escape. The river dries out at low tide. So I revisited the ancient castle, which, familiar to me since early childhood, I must have visited a dozen times or more. "This Castle was a Place of great Note in ye Saxon Times. It is in ye middle of ye Isle

NEWPORT

of Wight and was Anciently called Gavesburgh.
. . . This Castle has been remarkable lately for ye
confinement of King Charles I in It, till he was
removed to Hurst Castle." The last-named event
was " lately " in 1733 ; it is history now.

A maritime association with the castle is found in
the fact that from Carisbrooke Castle Sir G. Carey,

Governor of the Isle of Wight, wrote his account of the passing of the Armada. Under date of the 25th of July 1588 he recorded :

" This morning began a great fight betwixt both fleets south of the Island, which continued from five of the clock until ten, with so great expense of

FROM THE MEDINA — DURING REGATTA WEEK.                    6. AUGUST. 1925.

powder and bullet that during the said time the shot continued so thick together that it might rather have been judged a skirmish with small shot on land than a fight with great shot on sea. In which conflict, thanks be to God, there hath not been two of our men hurt. The fleets keep the direct Trade " (i.e. fairway of the Channel) " and shot into the sea out of our sight."

Back I went to my dinghy and made sail. Her wind free, the little boat flew back to Cowes in quick time on the racing ebb. I loitered along the front on the East Cowes side. Sunlight was bright upon the crowded anchorage, and on the royal yacht and her escort battleship. And then the huge rounded spinnakers of two of the big yachts appeared, milky white, as they got their guns in a close finish. I loitered, very well content ; the scene was full of beauty.

# CHAPTER VI

## INTO WOOTTON CREEK

THIS morning (for we had left Cowes a few days ago now) we found ourselves again off Seaview. Becalmed for the time being, we had let go our anchor somewhere off the pier head; and, on a light swell, the yacht rolled. The sun beat down on us. We pumped out the bilge, and made ourselves generally useful at any odd job that presented itself.

"The cabin gets a better sweeping out than usual." I was speaking from the cabin floor, where I was on my knees, dust-pan and brush in hand. "When the wind knocks off duty, the housework gets a chance."

After this we sat down and deservedly did nothing. Voices came over the water from miles away—the day was so still; and the seaside life of Seaview, with its bathing and paddling and sand-castles, carried on happily over there on the yellow sands in sunshine. As Mr. E. V. Lucas says:

> When August is here and our lessons are done
> The Island of Wight is the Island of fun.

A light breeze stirred at about two o'clock, due west. At the first breath we made sail, bound Solentwards.

" We're up against the east-going stream ; we'll have a job to make good at all over it."

We turned along the very edge of the Ryde Sand in order to cheat the tide as much as we could, and gradually we pushed on toward the Ryde Sand Head buoy. But there we were stopped by the tide ; we could not weather the buoy.

" The barge-type doesn't shine when asked to turn to windward over the tide," I commented ; I was sailing her very heedfully and doing my level best. " Now we'll see."

We stood off and on, just holding our own and no more. But, on this blue summer sea, we needed little philosophy to accept a mere delay. More philosophy was needed when one or two other yachts came up over the tide and weathered that very buoy which was quite beyond our own powers of achievement.

" They think we can't sail a boat," my shipmate complained. The touch of grievance was in his tone because he had fancied patronage in the glance of a passing helmsman. " But I dare say we'd make his little ship talk, if we'd got her," he added. She was a Solent class-boat, built for speed.

" I'd rather make her talk here than off St. Catherine's in a blow," I answered with complete equanimity. " Each for her own job."

Before long the full run of the tide had slackened, and we began to crawl over it, towards Ryde Pier.

Ryde, slightly larger than Newport, is in point of size the first town in the Island—unless the two

Cowes be counted as one. The town has little to suggest ancient origin, as it stands there looking northward over Spithead, for the houses and spires that build up behind the long railway pier are all modern. In position the town is a useful point of approach to the Island, standing as it does on a sheltered coast close to Portsmouth ; but there its natural advantages end, for it has no steep-to shore and no creek—nothing, in fact, to recommend it to the packet shipmasters of old days. Yet it became a port ; Rye or La Riche it was in 1340. When— under threat of French invasion—the trade and shipping of the Island were by Order concentrated during that year in three ports only, the three ports were La Riche, Shamblord (East Cowes), and Yarmouth. The first-named was burnt by the French shortly afterward.

The yacht went about close to the pier head, where a railway steamer was lying alongside ; a train, down the long pier, was puff-puffing its jet of steam, pure white against the silhouette of the town. There is an area, defined by buoys, in which no vessel is permitted to anchor, the object being to secure free access to the pier for the steamers. A channel about 120 yards wide is thus preserved.

Long though the pier is, it only just suffices to reach the sea at low water. The steamers, in fact, berth within rope's throw of the sand when the tide is out ; the sand is right aboard of them. Before the pier existed (it was first built in 1813) passengers from the Island, with their baggage, were taken in carts across the plashy stretch of sand, and sent

THE TRAIN ON RYDE PIER

off in a small boat to the sailing packet. A daily service between Ryde and Portsmouth (whether by sail or steam) has existed since 1796.

Few yachtsmen bring up off Ryde Pier. The breadth of the sand makes it necessary to take a berth well offshore, and the south-west wind knocks up quite a sea. The very look of the anchored vessels off Ryde has at times been sufficient argument for me, seeming as if they would almost roll their masts out; and quieter water can generally be found off Seaview or Osborne.

The tide was rising; and, after passing Ryde Pier, we beat close inshore for the mere pleasure of the sunlit landscape. It is a shore of modest slopes, well wooded.

Past Binstead, we were now off Quarr, once a place of consequence. It possessed a Benedictine monastery in 1132, and afterwards there was a great Cistercian abbey. Its abbot was " Warden of Wight." But Henry VIII and his " Hammer of the Monks " ended its story; the whole abbey was destroyed.

Our plans for the day had been entirely left in the air, but the pleasant appearance of Fishbourne, coupled with the lengthening of shadows on shore, suddenly hardened them.

" Let's go into Wootton."

The tide was high, and almost on the turn; no time must be lost if we were to enter. The appearance of the shore had changed since our last visit to the Solent, for the old perches had gone, and there are solid-looking dolphins which mark a dredged channel for railway cargo vessels conveying motor-cars to the island. By the lead we found that these dolphins must be left on the starboard side as one enters. On a long board the yacht sailed swiftly past them, but the tide was just beginning to stream out of Wootton, and it was touch and go whether she would be able to turn to windward up to a berth beyond the steamer quay.

" I'm not sure we haven't reckoned without our host," I said. " We're just a quarter of an hour late, and the tide's really on the move."

The channel is very narrow, and several yachts and other craft were at anchor. But *Growler* brought the thing off; and quite thankfully we heard the cable rattle down, for failure to get inside would have been a disappointment. Her sails were furled; she lay beside the trees, and her bows were soon parting the ebb-stream that was pouring in full body seaward from the creek.

The tide would allow time for us to explore the estuary up to Wootton Bridge, pulling up to it in the dinghy.

" Tons of time from every point of view," my shipmate added, as he looked into a saucepan. " The stew wants an hour or more."

We had set the stove going in the fo'c'sle, and we left the pot to simmer. Away we went up the little estuary between the trees.

Wootton Bridge is delightful from the water. The place is less attractive ashore, with its tarred road and its motor traffic. Motors (I speak as an offender) are the bane of the Island. We were glad to re-embark in the dinghy, and to loiter afloat below the tidemill. The old buildings were a picture; and, beyond the bridge, Ashey Down was distant in the low sunlight.

" Come on," I said at last ; and, with the ebb to help us, we were soon down to the yacht again.

I sniffed the air as we came up to leeward of her. " Really," I said, " if she gives the show away like this, we shall have to lock the hatches. What hungry tramp could resist such a smell ? "

We went on board, but the cook shook his head. " Give it half an hour longer," he said. So we took a turn ashore at Fishbourne, a pleasant old-world corner, though perhaps just a trifle too trim and self-conscious. The ebb was emptying so fast that we had a little work to get the dinghy floated as we returned. The shore is very flat.

In a comfortable frame of mind, we were on deck again half an hour later, washing up the crockery and enjoying the sunset and the light of the half moon. The wind had fallen to nothing, and the water had become as smooth as glass before nightfall.

Dark trees were imaged perfectly, and the reflected moon was yellow in the water. Not a sound disturbed the silence. Then, from far off, the light noise of a ripple breaking somewhere welled rather mysteriously along to us through the dusk, and it came nearer. A minute later all the yachts were set on the roll, and small waves were breaking, one after another, along the shores. The little turmoil, due to some liner that must have passed some time ago in the Solent, gradually

WOOTTON BRIDGE

subsided, and the images in the water were again perfect.

. . . . .

Morning had changed the mood of the creek when we turned out, for skies were clouded and a fresh wind was blowing. During this cruise we had made a contract—my shipmate and I—with regard to getting our anchor. My companion is not fond of handling that half-hundredweight mudhook; it is often filthy with mud—and must be coaxed on board, without violence and without damage to the paint, at a time when the decks are a-slope and slippery with water. I have not the smallest objection to the job myself; there are other tasks which I would infinitely rather forgo. I admit that I have no love of the cooking galley. Though ready for the job (and, I flatter myself, reasonably efficient at it), I am equally ready to slide out gracefully if I see an honest opportunity, and to let somebody else take over the pots, pans, and cooking-fork. So an unequal bargain has been struck—not at my suggestion, but my companion's. He undertakes to be ship's cook for the cruise provided that he is absolved from ever handling anchor or kedge. I should have absolved him on lighter terms had I not been tolerably certain that he really likes to squat there. He likes to put pinches of salt (with the wisest air conceivable) into some pot that simmers but must not boil. He prescribes with as much assurance and dignity as a doctor would prescribe in a serious case. Last night (for instance) his air was professorial when he prescribed an extra half-hour for that stew. But his results justify him ; and so I feel free to imagine that I am doing the right thing by him and the ship if—after setting the table—I loaf about in the well and look at the landscape while he is still bent double beside the stove. I have no qualm of conscience.

My own counter-labour is more rapidly discharged. This morning, too, my first bout of it was finished before his was begun, because, for reasons of tide, it was necessary to escape at once, and to breakfast out in the Solent. The anchor was " catted and fished " in quick time ; the wind was W.S.W. and plenty of it, so that we swung out of the creek more quickly than we had entered. As usual, we should have to turn to windward down the Solent ; it always happens. And we should probably do so in a dirty little seaway.

Inshore, in Osborne Bay, the water was smooth enough, and we sailed rapidly—accompanied, as it happened, by a school of porpoises. Idly we watched their movement, for they were breaking water close beside us all the time. They seldom rose singly ; usually they came up in pairs. Everybody is familiar with that curved outline of smooth and glossy back. The porpoises were so numerous to-day that, time after time, they rose in series, one pair following another and another.

" Look at it ! " My companion pointed. " Splash, splash, splash ; one, two, three, four ! Four loops of the same shiny back. Why, it's the sea-serpent ! "

The glossy curves did look really continuous, and

the same effect perhaps accounts for some of the
" veritable appearances " recorded.

Porpoises are very imperturbable folk in general,
and seem hardly to notice a small ship.   But on this
day one of the smooth-backed fellows really appeared
surprised when he broke surface very close to yacht.
He turned off, at a complete tangent from his
original course, and with a huge splash.   " Put the
wind up *him* for once," my shipmate laughed.

At the end of a board offshore, we passed the
*Mauretania*, outward bound by way of Spithead.
She was raising a monstrous wash.   The waves were
like the rounded seas of a big swell in the Channel ;
they far exceeded in dignity the natural waves of
the Solent.   When the great ship herself was away
beyond Ryde, we were still lifting and falling over
the heaped ridges of green sea.

Once clear of Old Castle Point we were at grips
with the characteristic seas of the Solent, steep and
vicious.   Full and bye, the yacht plugged to windward, and the waves smacked her, hard.   Her
flaring bows kept the sea pretty much in its place ;
very little green water had a chance of sluicing over
on the decks, but the spray came in showers.   She
punched on firmly ; and she might fancy that she
was back on her own East Coast.   This was the
precise little turmoil which she remembered in the
Blackwater or Crouch.   But the tide was still contrary, and we should lose little by anchoring for a
time in the shelter of Osborne Bay, thus getting our
breakfast in peace.   So we let go the anchor, and
went below for breakfast.

# CHAPTER VII

## PAST NEWTOWN TO YARMOUTH

AT turn of the tide we were away. The waves were breaking against the weather-going tide, and we thrashed to and fro out of Osborne Bay in a little lather of foam, while the dinghy flopped in the steep waves, tugging at its painters.

" Always a wet passage westward in the Solent."

Another of those whips of spray snapped across us. The green-grey water looked chilly and unfriendly, and the distances were a trifle grim. The whole seascape was dour under low clouds; the waves, as they topped to sudden foam-crests, had a touch of menace.

Then for one moment the clouds rifted somewhere, and let through a single shaft of sunlight. The glitter of light was like a charm; the whole seascape was brought to life by it. After that, gradually, the clouds became detached masses of white on a sky of blue. The wind had not moderated and the weight of the seas was unchanged, but the waves lost their vicious look at once. Under blue skies they were no longer formidable, and the spray which still swept us at moments had lost its sting.

The broken cliffs of Gurnard, covered with thickets, were close aboard of us just now, golden in sunlight. We turned to windward through the Solent, patiently winning our way.

" There's Newtown River," I said at last, pointing to a line of silver behind a low spit. We had just made a long board inshore.

We were not entering to-day. We should only have the one glimpse, for the upper reaches were lost in wooded landscape inland, towards the grey background of down.

The river is a pleasant place in which to anchor. I recall more than one summer day when, anchored inside, I have explored its lakes in the dinghy, and I have also sojourned there for a long spell. " Lakes " they call the creeks. I have explored each separate spur of the inlet. There are Clamerkin Lake, Western Haven, Shalfleet Lake, Corf Lake and Causeway Lake. The last-named leads to Newtown, and Shalfleet Lake to a mill and road close to the village of Shalfleet where

> Poor and simple Shalfleet people,
> Sold their bells to build a steeple.

They sold their bells and the church gun in order to get money to erect a wooden spire on the square tower of the church ; but the wooden spire has been discarded again now. The place is ancient, and figures in the *Domesday Book* as Seldeflet.

A pleasant contrast, I have found it, on a summer's evening, after perhaps a rough passage outside, to come to anchor in Newtown, and to stroll up these wooded lanes, in the evening light, to the farm-yards and thatched cottages.

Newtown itself is, of course, no mere ordinary

village, but a place with a history. It was once Francheville, the free town, and is said to have been the capital of the Island. Built beside a tidal estuary well suited to the needs of mediæval and earlier times, it prospered. It had been sacked by the Danes in 1001 (its name was probably then Wealtham), but it was again in full tide of prosperity when it was granted its charter of incorporation by Henry III. Edward II also granted it a charter for a three days' annual fair, vigil, and feast. Ships of 500 tons burden were able to use the haven, and the place was a notable port. Then, in 1377, the French sacked and burnt it, and destroyed it utterly.

After lying desolate, the site was again used for a new town ; but the place is now the merest of villages, and its " Quay Street," " Drapers' Alley," and " High Street," once thronged by merchants of the Middle Ages, are fieldways or country lanes. No one appears to know quite definitely whether the place was destroyed for a third time or whether it has merely decayed. There is remarkably little left now. Francheville has quite vanished, and the Newtown which followed it has almost vanished too.

From the Solent, Newtown River looked like a silver lake, landlocked there ; at the end of the next board inshore we were opposite Bouldnor Cliff, and Newtown River was a thing of the past. The wooded cliffs look very attractive. Once, when the yacht was anchored in Newtown, I tried a walk along the foot of them, but I found it very bad going indeed. The cliffs were less picturesque, too, from that angle.

The wind had now taken off; oilskins had been discarded, and sunshine was genial.

"A wonderful expedition, always, when one sets one's face towards the open. . . ." I was saying it

JACK-IN-THE-BASKET AND HURST CASTLE

somewhere in the neighbourhood of the Solent Banks buoy. The tide was helping us westward at speed, and would carry us out past the Needles, if we chose, before it turned. Why not?

NIGHT IN WOOTTON CREEK

THE NARROWS OF THE
SOLENT OFF HURST CASTLE

The Solent, to eastward of Hurst Castle, is like a broad river ; but beyond Hurst it is the sea. Let us escape, then, even if we had to return at once. The expedition at once became a voyage of discovery. The prospect beyond this narrow sea-gate seems somehow to be found and discovered anew at every time of passage. Grey in sunward haze, the familiar outline of Hurst Castle was visible ; Bouldnor had gone by the southward side, and Yarmouth Pier and Church were nearer. At half-past six they were abeam.

" It means coming back into Yarmouth in the dark," I reflected ; " but this is too splendid." It had to be done.

In the gut between Cliff End and Hurst Castle the waves were breaking right across the fairway just as if the whole thing were a belt of shoal. They always do, when this tide, at four to five and a half knots, goes sluicing through, and the wind from the south-west is blowing stiffly against it.

" Look out for it now ! " my companion chuckled, and he grabbed an oilskin. So also did I, and none too soon, for the spray raked us in showers that rattled. The yacht rose and plunged, thrashed and toppled ; but the disturbance was shortlived, and —the narrows once passed—she was soon working through her channel in a quieter fashion.

Drayton, as already quoted, spoke of the rudeness of those " irefull Tides " that " upon the bulwarkt Forts of *Hurst* and *Calsheot* beat." In point of fact, the tides beat much more rudely upon Hurst than upon Calshot. With the prevailing south-west

wind, there is almost always something of a lop off
Hurst.

Low sunlight, full in our eyes, glowed upon the
earthy cliffs of Colwell and Totland as we left them
astern. We took care to locate the Shingles buoys
and to leave the line of them well to northward
each time ; the shoal is more than three miles long
—one mass of yellow shingle, a small portion of
which uncovers. The Admiralty *Channel Pilot*
gives it the bad reputation which it deserves.
" Caution " (says the book) " is requisite in approaching this shoal on either side, for the rapidity of the
tidal streams and the violence with which the sea
curls and breaks with the least swell over the
numerous shallow heads entails almost certain
destruction to any vessel driven on it."

As day dropped to evening the full magic of the
western Solent was ours. The broken slopes, with
their woods and thickets, become trivial when the
smooth curves of downland rise distantly beyond
them. Gradually, more and still more, the long
down rises and dominates everything. Those earthy
cliffs finish ; and, as the yacht sails westward, there
is the great down only, with its sheer drop of flint-
ribbed chalk, perpendicular to the sea, in Alum
Bay.

Flushed, as it faced the sunset, the huge cliff held
us in silent awe. The yacht was still beating westward, close under its shadow, and we handled the
sheets without a word—fairly enthralled by the
wonder of that rose-bathed chalk. The cliff towered
above us, taciturn, primeval, almost fabulous.

PAST COLWELL TO THE NEEDLES

Then, as the failing tide-stream carried us westward with its last life, we drew away from the landfall, and the Needles rocks were passed. Evening
was on us. The Island lay astern, seeming to swim
in a haze of twilight; the flush was still there,
fading gradually. In the late dusk, we put up the
helm, and the mainsheet was run out through the
blocks. With a breeze that had fallen lighter, we
barely held way against the last of the tide; but
true on course the yacht remained, pointed Solent-
ward again, and bound for the Needles Channel.
The lighthouse flashed, and we hung poised between
wind and tide, while the Island paled to a sober
grey, and was now dull-hued, but very noble still,
in the nightfall.

"We'll walk over those downs to-morrow," I

said.   I seem to know every hump and hollow, and
the lure of them—seen in this twilight—was not to
be denied.

The tide slackened and turned.   In light winds
in particular one must remember the dictum of
Grenville Collins, which, true in 1692, is equally
true now : " The Tyde of Ebb setteth on the
*Shingles*, which are hard stones.   The Flood setteth
on the *Needles*."   With the flood we again passed
the Needles, giving them a berth, and passed by
the chalk face, now grey in the dark, to Alum Bay.
There are some detached rocks, under water, off
Heatherwood Point, and a ledge off Warden Point ;
the shore at the Points must not, therefore, be
approached too closely.   Thus we entered the
Narrows again.   Hurst light was flashing, and we
were in the Solent.   Shaping course for Yarmouth,
care was needed to avoid the Black Rock ; rocks at
that spot uncover at low tide ; they are buoyed but
not lighted.   In daylight the buoy can be passed
at close quarters, but at night—in a light breeze—
there is a spice of mild anxiety.   If one stood too
close one might find the rocks in a fashion very much
undesired ; whereas, if the berth given were too
generous, the strong tide might hurry the yacht
past Yarmouth Pier before she could make her haven,
and return would then be impossible until change of
tide.

Neither trouble materialised in fact, and the
yacht, level with the red light on the pier head, was
reaching in towards the harbour.   The leading
lights are supposed to be green and white ; actually

they were (at this time) unashamedly white, just like a couple of ordinary street lamps. But we picked them up without trouble, and were soon in, rounding the right-angled bend behind the break-water.

The whole place was asleep; no anchor lights need to be shown, and everything is moored stem and stern, as is the custom of the port. The flood was under us, and we crept up by gradual degrees. The hour was midnight.

Dark though it was, we had no difficulty in locating the channel, and we could see pretty well what space of water was available for manœuvre. The tide was low. At high water it is much more deceptive, for the posts are a long way out of place. Far in on the mud, they were high and dry now. A patch of oozy bank stretched between them and the water's edge. We made fast in a vacant mooring.

In the darkness the little harbour was primitive and mediæval. A small town of huddled roofs clustered by the waterside, and the ramparts of a castle loomed above the moored vessels. The rig of the ships was indistinguishable; they might have been cogs and carracks, rounded little tubs of ships such as that in which King John embarked in 1206 from this port for Rochelle, having ordered that all ships capable of carrying eight horses or more should be taken up and manned. The expedition itself assembled at Southampton.

Expeditions did not assemble at Yarmouth; it has always been a port of small things. Even now

Yarmouth is the smallest parish in the Isle of Wight, containing only fifty-eight acres, but it is one of the oldest boroughs. And its river and sheltered position gave it importance as a place of approach for the Island either by friend or enemy. Henry VIII fortified it with the castle, part of which remains ; and a portion of that castle stands upon the wall of a church which had been demolished by the French in some obscure raid of the dim Middle Ages.

Small though the port was, its roadstead was much used, giving as it did immediate shelter from south-westerly winds. Fleets also lay here, as sailing vessels still lie, waiting for a wind. The number of sailing vessels which have lain windbound in the roadstead must be beyond number. In 1783, a young sailor, while on anchor watch here in one of them, wrote that he " heard a flock of Solan geese on a calm night making a noise like a pack of hounds."

" Time to turn in," I yawned, as I made the last warp fast and looked around appreciatively at the darkness. " The tide's rising now ; look at it." The water was welling up over the flat banks apace. But it was too late to linger. We turned in.

. . . . .

In the morning light the town was as primitive as ever, utterly remote from the twentieth century. The little breakwater was simple entirely, the old bridge was a bridge that men might have made when the castle walls—mossy and ancient now— were first built by the Tudor king. The whole scene basked in sunshine.

KING JOHN SAILS FROM YARMOUTH IN 1206.

The hand of change has since been rather heavy, for the old bridge has gone already, and the harbour is to be dredged and modernised. The new bridge —though less acceptable than the old one—is not unsightly.

Under the bridge the tidal river leads to Freshwater, and is navigable at high water in the dinghy, with views that are everywhere a picture—the reed-bordered river, the copses, and the downs beyond. I have loitered up and down it at all hours, morning, noon, and night.

In the holiday month of August cruising yachts will often make prolonged stay in this pleasant harbour of Yarmouth, where the sheltered moorings are just beside the Solent, and a little sandy shore is at hand, for the cruising youngsters.

Days, and nights, could hardly be more acceptably spent than afloat like this. Southward, the long line of the downs is seen, northward is the traffic of the Solent. That traffic (I have to admit) is of less interest now than when I was a child, because the greatest liners have abandoned the Solent passage in favour of Spithead ; but there is much astir still. Standing on the deck of the yacht, one watches the ships pass, and sees the lights of them in the night-time. Then, long after the ocean-bound steamship has gone by, the wash from her is splashing along the breakwater and slopping over between the posts. At extreme high water the wash will set the yachts rolling, just as—at high water—a north-east wind will send a swell into the harbour. But apart from that, and at all other times, the moored vessels lie completely sheltered.

Nothing can disturb them, unless perhaps their sanctuary is once in a way invaded by some collier steamer with a cargo for the gas-works that are hidden out of sight somewhere beyond the bridge.

FRESHWATER FROM THE RIVER YAR

The space for her is narrow, and she has two right-angled corners to turn inside the harbour. The steamer enters with a bevy of eager row-boats about her, and the skipper of every yacht is probably holding his biggest fenders in readiness as she comes slowly by, " in case."

The only other invader of Yarmouth Harbour in holiday time is the common wasp. And the common wasp is a perfect nuisance. One cannot enjoy one's well-earned meal to the tune of so much concentrated buzzing at such close quarters. The only simple alternative is often invoked. Every wasp is slaughtered or chased into the open, and the skylight is closed and the cabin battened down until the meal is over, too little air being much better than too many wasps.

A whole chapter could be written upon the tragic subject of wasps.

> They pingle round your head—
> The black-and-yellow monoplanes,
> The come-and-go-and-come-agains
> That kill a picnic dead.

If the yacht is much at anchor in wasp-frequented places the nuisance can be met by stretching muslin over skylight and well. This plan was followed with great success by a well-known cruising yachtsman.

But on one occasion the plan worked quite the wrong way round. The yachtsman was obliged to be away from his yacht one whole hot summer's day at Pin Mill, and, rather than let his cabin become an oven (as it would have become if battened down

THE OLD TOLL-BRIDGE AT YARMOUTH (RECENTLY REPLACED)

under the hot sunlight) he left it open, but left the muslin carefully set to guard it against the wasps.

He returned after nightfall. All was quiet and dark in the cabin, and he lit a lamp and began to set about getting a little supper. He opened his grocery locker ; and the moment the beam of lamp-light entered it there was a great concentrated *buzz*. Two solid masses of wasps, each mass as big as a man's fist, were sleeping there, and they were all beginning to stir in the lamplight. He closed the locker in a hurry.

Another locker he had, near the well, and to that he turned. Another great mass of wasps was there, which also began to stir and buzz. He shut that also with a snap, and sat down to think.

What had happened was obvious. The wasps had found some little hole in the muslin through which they could enter, and then—having forgotten it—had been unable to leave the cabin when, at dusk, all well-behaved wasps flit away home to the nest to sleep. They had been caught exactly as lobsters are caught in a lobster-pot, and there were hundreds of them.

If released suddenly now they might think they had a grudge against their host, a chance which he was not disposed to accept. So he did some hard thinking. At last he remembered that he had heard somewhere that, if a candle in a basin of water is put in among them, they will singe their wings in the flame and so drop and drown themselves in the water. He found two candles and put them in two basins, lit them up in the lockers, fastened the doors carefully, and turned in.

The plan was completely successful. Both basins were piled so high with dead wasps in the morning that the candles had been extinguished with their bodies. Very few wasps indeed were left alive. Having thus decimated the local wasp population, he sailed away, determined that both his muslin net and his locker doors should be a better fit next time !

# CHAPTER VIII

## TO LYMINGTON AND BEAULIEU

THERE was sunshine on Yarmouth Harbour, but clouds were low on the downs. Beyond the old toll-bridge, the Yar led towards the downs and Freshwater ; but the tide was ebbing, and we could not reach them by way of the river. We must go by land ; so we pulled across to the stone steps of the quay. If the wind happens to be vigorous from the northward, full into the harbour mouth, those stone steps at once become a difficult landing, for the waves will be washing up three or four slippery steps at a time, while the dinghy will be bobbing up cork-like on each wave, and dropping with equal suddenness. It will, in fact, show itself as lively as only a dinghy—beside a fixed object—can. Without sea-boots it is a work of art to get ashore dry-shod. But the wind was gentle to-day and westerly, and the harbour was like a mill-pond. I tied up the dinghy.

The harbour-side remains unchanged, with its old stone-built square beside the ancient castle, and the little office for the harbour-master.

We went through the square fronting the church and town hall. The motor-cars and motor-coaches now assemble at all sorts of hours in the square, meeting the steamers, and they are—to my own eye —horribly out of the picture. One remembers that square, with the old Freshwater coach, horse-drawn, and generally also a shabby victoria or two —all primitive as the old square itself.

We made our way to Freshwater by train, and from Freshwater Station we shaped our course for the downs. Up over the sheep-trimmed turf, we went to the highest point of Freshwater Down, where I used in childhood to hear the wind whistle

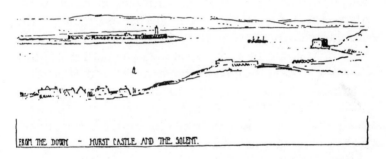

FROM THE DOWN - HURST CASTLE AND THE SOLENT.

in the old Nodes Beacon. The Tennyson cross is there now.

The Island below us, and the Solent beyond it, were spread out almost plan-like. From this down, it is Hurst Castle and Cliff End and the Shingles that we see; from Afton, it is Yarmouth and the winding Yar; from Shalcombe and Mottistone, Newtown River is seen in plan. The whole terrain to me is full of memories; in silence we paced down over the cropped sward, and then along the lanes.

Back again at Yarmouth, we were busy at once. It was past four in the afternoon, and the day's sailing was yet to be done. Keyhaven, Lymington, and Beaulieu River—we had hoped to revisit all three to-day, for just a flying glimpse; the first named we were ready to relinquish on this occasion as we were so late in starting, but that only. We were ready.

"Yarmouth has seen me in scrapes before now," I confessed, "but I fancy it won't to-day."

The little harbour can be strangely awkward to enter or leave, with its sharp elbow-bend and scanty space; and, as a fellow sailing-man once complained: "There's always a row of old men on the old bench up there; they do nothing but watch the ships come in and out and say what the fellows handling them ought to have done and haven't." I think he must have piled up his own little hooker, under gaze of that critical gallery, for he spoke with mild venom: "Doddering old fools!" he added, "they'd be the first to take the putty themselves."

But in that, I fancy, he did them less than justice. For knowledge of these Solent tides is more than half the battle; and the tides are full of tricks. The chief and obvious eccentricity of the tides is their double high water; but that by no means is the only one. The tide will flow briskly a while and then linger, quite stationary, for a bout, gathering strength for its next effort. The periods are calculable, and the old hands exploit the slack moments. The stranger, on the other hand, may readily bungle matters. He will try to escape from harbour against a racing flood tide and will fail; but the battered habitué, pipe in mouth, is waiting just half an hour longer, and will then sail forth successfully, a picture of unconcern. Half an hour later still, the flood tide will be sluicing in again as if its flow had never been interrupted. The whole thing is a riddle to the unlearned.

To-day, however, we need not wait upon the tide; it was ebbing, and the wind was fair. Our foresail alone would carry us out to freedom, and away we went, setting the mainsail at leisure when we had gained the open Solent. Course was laid —as the railway steamer lays it—for Jack-in-the-Basket, allowing for drift of tide; the wind was on our beam and we steered a straight course. A great Dutch liner, towering from the water, crossed our bows just comfortably distant, so that there was no need for us to change course for her. But we were just in time to involve ourselves with her wash. The liner was already beginning to work up her ocean speed, and her wash was mountainous.

" Leaving us something to remember her by," my companion laughed, as he steadied himself against the flying gunwale, and looked at the retreating hull with its cloud of smoke.

Our one regretful glance was towards Hurst shingle-bank, behind which lies Keyhaven. The long creek called Keyhaven Lake has a shallow bar, but there are good depths inside. One or two spurs of it lose themselves in mere mud, but Keyhaven Lake reaches solid Hampshire. There is little at the waterside save a quay more than half ruined and a few small boats. The creek-head wears an air of desertion now, but Keyhaven was once a port of some pretensions.

The charm of Keyhaven Lake is that it affords an anchorage in such complete shelter within a stone's throw of the open. Waves may be breaking in fury on the other side of Hurst shingle-bank, but the creek will be calm. The only drawback is that the mud is soft, and anchors are inclined to drag.

This place—with its landlocked basin at mouth of the creek—is very satisfying after a rough passage. My recollections of anchorage in Keyhaven are singularly pleasant. I remember one evening in particular when I arrived just at sunset. As evening darkened, one listened, with a sense of security and comfort, to the booming of the waves, and watched the lights of Hurst (just at hand) and the Needles over the Bank.

Not only was the anchored yacht safe from the sea there, she was also safe from the traffic. I was startled into wakefulness (I remember) after a dreamless night by the foghorn of a liner—a sound which seemed positively in my ear, so close it was. And the liner was in fact remarkably close as she passed, just at the other side of the shingle-bank. I tumbled out in a hurry. Nothing at all was visible, because mist was everywhere. A red glow of dawn was just tinging the mist pink.

During a quiet summer morning the dinghy sailed up to Keyhaven for provisions—a usual programme.

Almost the whole of the end of the shingle-bank

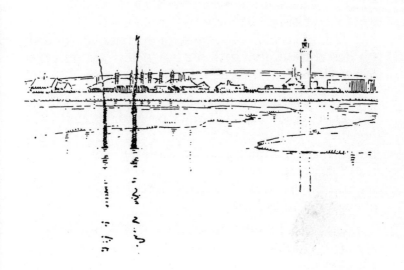

IN KEYHAVEN LAKE

on its outer side is steep-to. One can land at any state of the tide, and loiter about by the castle walls. No one else seems to do so ; I have always had the place to myself. Recently notices have been erected ; but at all events the shore below high-water mark cannot be closed.

Hurst Castle is a fine landmark, if nothing else. Built of naked stone on an open bank of shingle, it would be finished at once by a modern shell or two, but it has been a commanding fortress in its day. Its description, quaintly set out below an old print of two hundred years ago, is thus written :

" This Castle was built by King Henry VIII for the Defence of that Channel or Passage call'd the Needles. It is a narrow neck of land shooting out beyond the mainland of Hampshire, commanding the Sea every way. And is also over against Yarmouth in the Isle of Wight, where the sea is not above two miles over."

Henry VIII built Hurst Castle of material from Beaulieu Abbey. What little now remains of his original structure bears the date 1535. In the reign of Mary there was an attempt to betray the castle to the French, but the plot was discovered and the traitor executed. Then, years later, Charles I was detained in it for eighteen days in very close confinement—in a wretched closet eight feet by four feet six inches.

That long shingle ridge, like in kind with Chesil Bank, is a feature of the western Solent. The theory is that the stony material drifted from the

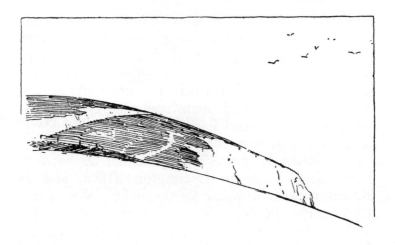

THE CURVE OF THE DOWN

westward during the ages, ready to bring up upon
any obstacle. The muddy shallows that front
Keyhaven and Lymington were sufficient, and here
the great breakwater built itself. The Shingles
Shoal, already mentioned, is probably of like origin,
and the belief is that it banked itself there—in mid
channel—on a rocky foundation, because the tide
on one side is so much swifter than that on the side
opposite.

Jack-in-the-Basket was now over the bows of the
yacht, and the whole regiment of booms and withies
that mark the Lymington River. Two red lights
up in Lymington give the line of approach at night
from the Solent, and four marks in the river are
lighted. These latter lights are attended twice

weekly, and I have seen some of them in great need of it—showing a glimmer only, not to be discerned at all unless one were actually searching them out. The fixed marks themselves are—by daylight—picturesque, with their distinctive little bits of top-hamper, and some of them have their own names, such as " Tar Barrel Boom " and " Cocked Hat." The river is plain sailing.

Our idea to-day was merely to sail up between these tidal banks to Lymington Town, and to return, without stopping for the night. We wanted only another passing glimpse of its ancient township and the familiar reaches of its river. It is on the borders of the New Forest, where the wooded country-side comes down to the water's edge ; and —anchored here—I have lain awake in the cabin and heard the nightingales half the night long. Lifting one's self on one elbow from the bunk, and looking through the porthole, one has seen a glitter of moon-light, and has turned drowsily over, to fall asleep again to the tune of the nightingales.

On some other quiet night here the mist had gathered early and made everything spectral. A yacht moored close to *Growler* was a dark blur upon the mist, but otherwise the whole world was a wraith and a shadow. I turned in, alone. Again there were the nightingales, and I could also hear the foghorns of steamers that searched their way up or down the Solent. Two of them were trying to locate one another, feeling their way ; the deep booming of a great ship being answered by the bleat-bleat of some tramp, and again by a low booming from another quarter. The Needles station, somewhere in the background, had a separate note of its own at regular intervals. Then —sleepless just now—I put out my head into a night that was weird and ghostly. I could hear the anxious ships' bells, from two vessels which I had seen bring up inside the Lymington Banks in the afternoon. And—on the landward side—the nightingales were still singing.

I dropped to sleep, and awakened to sound of the cuckoo. But there was no glow of sunshine, low through the mist, giving promise of a fine day. The mist had gone. I was out washing down the decks under a low sky of huddled cloud. The Island looked much too close for fine weather ; every building at Yarmouth was plainly outlined, and the chalk pits on Freshwater Down and the white cliff between Alum and the Needles were cut with quite undue precision. A day followed of rain in spate which drove me to the cabin, for no breath of wind was abroad ; the rain was pattering on the skylight ; on the flat water, when I looked out, were the thousand-thousand spot-spots of rain unceasing. One solitary seagull was standing on a post. Otherwise, I was quite alone.

These trivial memories have no bearing on the present expedition, but they are somehow part and parcel of Lymington. And another trifle which it has amused me to watch is the happening of the wash of the steamer. Passing along the narrow ditch at low tide, the steamers look substantial vessels for such a mud trickle ; but actually they only draw some five feet of water. When the tidal mud is just awash, and only just, the effect is most noticeable. A regular cataract of water runs *off* the flats to meet the steamer, uncovering again the mud-banks which the flood tide had hidden half an hour ago ; then the breaking wave returns and throws the anchored dinghies this way and that on the mud, and surges up to the stone-built wall itself. The same out-suck and return wave have broken much crockery on board the unsuspecting yachts of strangers—despite the care of the packet skippers, who are consideration itself. I was hearing of such a case the other day. The yacht had just anchored and was snugly afloat at edge of the tideway. It happened that tea had been set on the cabin table. Then came the steamer. Suddenly the out-wash put the yacht aground, listing her over on one side ; then the return wave threw her over on the other side. All the crockery was on the cabin floor—in pieces.

The long mud flats, more than a mile wide here, between the solid shore and the Solent, are never completely covered save at the highest spring tides. The coarse, brown, stubbly grasses that clothe them are of a kind seldom met elsewhere—or so they assure me locally. It is said that a rice ship was wrecked here years ago and its cargo lost. The rice germinated, and a coarse type of degenerate rice, crossed perhaps with other strains of plant-life, spread broadcast.

We sailed up past the Railway Pier to the old town's quay and ferry. Visited ashore the High

HENRY II ARRIVING AT LYMINGTON

Street, on its hill, is particularly pleasing. And the place is full of history. The town was a Roman station once, and residence of a British king. It was granted a charter in 1150; the charter was confirmed by Queen Elizabeth. In 1154 King Henry II landed here, having narrowly escaped drowning on his voyage, and twelve days later he was crowned at Westminster ; for, at that time, the town was a seaport of serious claims. But in 1324 it drew upon itself the wrath of its great neighbour, Southampton, because it had begun to exact dues from shipping. Shipping dues were always a bone of contention ; and Southampton took action, with the result that the limits of the senior port were defined as embracimg the whole coast from Hurst to Langston.

In 1345 began the campaign of Crecy. Ships were demanded, from all ports in proportion to their wealth and substance. The local figures are interesting : Southampton, 21 ; Lymington, 9 ; Portsmouth, 5.

Down the river again we sailed in a brisk breeze, beating only through one reach, down to " Cocked Hat." In that reach it was that the steamer met us ; but the tide was high and the space was sufficient.

So we cleared the river, and the sunlight was on the water behind Jack-in-the-Basket.

" Look at the dancing glitter," my companion said, as he shaded his eyes, turning westward. " It's real high summer."

" We're leaving a land of dreams," I echoed regretfully, as I put the helm up and brought the long line of downs over the starboard quarter and the Needles astern. " Good is to come," I said, " but none better."

The wind, south-west, was on this course dead over the stern, a position not desired.

" This doesn't make for happiness," I said. " If we bring the wind decisively upon one quarter or the other we needn't be watching her all the time like a cat watches a mouse. I don't like sailing at constant edge of a gybe."

So we laid our course for Newtown ; I put her straight at the line of low cliff that basked in sunlight. Having no spinnaker, we rigged out a couple of headsails to do duty—for the strong Solent stream was contrary.

There is a regular little race off Hamstead Ledge, and the waves were breaking against the tide, shoreward of the buoy. Here we gybed and laid course for Beaulieu River.

" Day's getting on," said my shipmate, looking at the sun.

Yes, it was nearly seven.

" We shall be entering Beaulieu in the dark if the wind eases at all," I replied.

Twilight had fallen before we brought the East Lepe buoy abeam, and our makeshift spinnakers had been handed. We were reaching in, and the failing light made the coastguard houses indistinguishable until we were close to the entrance. In fact, we recoiled once, for the lead—kept going as we approached—had shown too rapid a shoaling ; and I could not see. But at last I made out the buildings. The white boat-house, if kept well towards the west end of the line of coastguard houses, gives an entrance. By daylight the course so set enables the leading marks to be located. Once in, the perches on the spit are sufficient guide, and they showed up to-night like sentinels in the grey glimmer, with wavered reflections below them in the shallows. The wind held, but darkness was complete before we had brought Bull-lake and Needs Oar abeam, and midnight was nearly upon us when we had made good our way to Bucklers Hard. The old houses were just to be seen on the hill-side, with not one glimmer of light at any window.

Seen by day they have quite a singular aspect, those two long rows with the wide, grassy space between them. Everybody comments upon this street, so strangely wide, but not everybody who comments remembers the reason. The street was made unusually wide to accommodate the huge stacks of timber for the shipbuilding yard below.

The first house on the right-hand side (at the back of it I have more than once bought a loaf in times gone by) was the house of master-builder Adams, born in 1713. He died in 1805, the year of Trafalgar, at the age of ninety-two. When, in 1789, the seventy-four *Illustrious* was launched at Bucklers Hard, it was said that "this makes the twenty-first of the line that Mr. Adams has built at Bucklers Hard, besides which he has built as many more at other places." Three of the Bucklers Hard ships of the line fought at Trafalgar—the *Agamemnon*, *Swiftsure*, and *Euryalus*.

Nelson's *Agamemnon* was the most famous of the Bucklers Hard ships. Her history is well known; it is perhaps less well known nowadays that—in her prime—she bore the nickname of "Old Eggs and Bacon."

MOONRISE AT BUCKLERS HARD

Captain Horatio Nelson, then aged thirty-four, was appointed to *Agamemnon* in 1793, and he commanded her in the Nelsonian manner, so that, when she went into dock at Leghorn to refit, " there was not a mast, yard, sail, or any part of the rigging, but what stood in need of repair, having been cut to pieces with shot. The hull was so damaged that it had for some time been secured by cables, which

were served or thrapped round it." " Poor
*Agamemnon,*" Nelson had said, " was as nearly
worn out as her captain ; and both must soon be
laid up for repair." It was when in command of
the *Agamemnon* that Nelson lost his eye.

The *Agamemnon* was afterwards at Copenhagen
(where she went aground on the edge of a shoal
when second in the line) as well as at Trafalgar.

The amount of wood required for a ship of the
line was immense. For one ship of 1,300 tons the
felling of 2,000 oak trees was necessary. A ship also
required 100 tons of wrought iron and 30 tons of
copper. The usual practice was for the men-of-war
built at Bucklers Hard to be taken to Portsmouth
to be coppered.

The New Forest was close about us. We could
somehow feel the neighbourhood of it, pleasantly,
during the night, with its sensation of dark glades
and woodland smells. I (as it happened) was out
watching the dark landscape over the river more
than was strictly needful, for a minor accident had
occurred. Coming to anchor, I had held a little
too far toward shore in the darkness, and had taken
the mud. It did not really matter an atom ; I had
laid out an anchor into the deeper water, and she
would float herself off to it, unwatched. But I had
the thing on my conscience, and I knew that I
should sleep the better when I had seen her anchored
in the fairway, her cable shortened to a few fathoms.
For that reason I turned out twice into the darkness ; and, as I waited, the forest-land and the
silence were with me.

There must have been cruel times for the country-side when the Chase was originally cleared, and the roof-trees of the peasants were everywhere levelled by the Conqueror. " He loved the wild deer as though he had been their father. Whoever should slay hart or hind, man should blind him."

Camden, writing of the " Newforest," recorded that " Walter Mapes who lived near the time says : ' the Conqueror took away the ground from God and man to dedicate it to wild beasts and sport of dogs ; in which he destroyed 36 mother churches, and ruined the inhabitants of their parishes.' "

Up river to-night all was darkness ; not a light was anywhere to indicate the position of the ancient village and abbey of Beaulieu. The site was such a one as the Cistercians loved, with its deep woods and tidal river. A quay at Beaulieu still shows the work of the monks, and the remains of the Abbey are now piously preserved.

Before its suppression, that great abbey must have dominated the landscape. It was completed in 1246, and dedicated in the presence of Henry III and a great retinue of nobles. But its founder was King John. And a story is told about the foundation, perhaps a legend which popular tradition felt obliged to create in order to account for an act of piety from so unexpected a quarter. For King John was no pillar of the Church. Having—or so the story runs- -some complaint against the Cistercian abbots, the King ordered the abbots to attend him at Lincoln. Then he let his temper get the better of him, and threatened to have them trodden by wild horses. But that very night he dreamed, and his dream was a nightmare. He found himself before a great judge, and all the abbots were ranged there, each with an accusing finger pointed at him. This great judge then handed him over to the abbots with command that he could be soundly scourged on his bare back. The abbots evidently laid on with a will, so that the King's back and shoulders ached with it when he awoke. In a panic, he sent for his chaplains, and he founded Beaulieu Abbey in expiation.

Thus it was, they say, that the great pile of monastic buildings arose. Its Angelus would ring, musical across the wooded country-side ; its white-habited community formed a regular township of their own. And Beaulieu was a sanctuary which retained its virtue long after other sanctuaries had lost their security. To Beaulieu it was that Ann Neville, wife of " The Kingmaker," fled in 1471 when Warwick had been slain at Barnet. In 1497 Perkin Warbeck claimed sanctuary there ; he surrendered on promise of life, but was perfidiously executed at Tyburn all the same.

In the darkness I had lingered now for quite a long time, alone. I bestirred myself, and felt my way for'ard, to give a haul on the cable. It came freely. *Growler* was afloat, and I shortened the chain and went below.

Above Bucklers Hard the river shallows, but Beaulieu can still be reached—by dinghy for pre-ference if the yacht draws much water. But there is also a path through the covers, skirting the

IN YARMOUTH HARBOUR

SETTING SAIL FROM KEYHAVEN

ecclessia sanctae mariae de

bello loco regis a.d. mcciv

BEAULIEU ABBEY IN THE OLDEN TIME

riverside, which in season is nothing less than a delight. It is most perfect perhaps in April, when the ground is a mass of bluebells and primroses and the covers have not yet become dense with their curtain of summer green. Spidery stems, and foliage budding like a green haze, give mystery to the distance, and the gleam of the river shines through. The cuckoo will no doubt be calling somewhere in the woodland.

# CHAPTER IX

## SOUTHAMPTON

WIND was light and the morning grey. We were anchored in the heart of the New Forest; gorse straggled to the water's edge beside us, and the fringe of grey larches made a jagged skyline. This was a real solitude.

"It's a pity," said my shipmate, as his eye followed the silver track of some water-fowl across the river.

"It is," I responded, catching the drift of his thought. "We're out of the world here, and Southampton—isn't."

But we wanted to be stirring. Our homage to the ideal of silence and solitude to-day was lip service only. We made sail.

We had coiled down the last of the halyards, and I was lolling at the helm.

"Lazy going to-day," I said to my shipmate. He, like me, was a picture of idleness, as he lay full length, his eyes upon the dark green reflections under the trees; and we were both happy to be under way!

Down this quiet river the yacht stole seaward, with a wind that breathed—it was little more than a breath—from the south-west. From Needs Oar the breeze gave us a long reach, and then we beat out over the bar, making short boards into the Solent.

" Watch the leading marks astern ; don't let me open them out too much either way. Then we needn't use the lead."

It was slow work ; we had broken out our anchor at half-past nine, and one o'clock had come and gone before we had brought Calshot Castle abeam. That castle (Calshot now, once Coldshore) was built in 1536, as part of a system of defence of the harbour against pirates.

The breeze, such as it was, had become a fair wind now that we were in Southampton Water. Southampton Water is one of the finest natural harbours of the Kingdom. With the Isle of Wight set athwart its opening to the English Channel, the whole harbour is landlocked, and no sea of consequence to ordinary shipping can be raised, even in the heaviest gales. It has one drawback, all the same, for its entrance is very limited ; a broad shoal —the Brambles Bank—is set straddled across the opening. The channel that enters the harbour is narrow ; it has been deepened to thirty-two feet, and is kept open by dredging.

Here it was that the wind deserted us altogether. Even in the most crowded lanes of shipping a yacht is well able to take care of herself, provided only that a breeze, however light, is allowed her. Without it she drifts quite helplessly. And at this point, where the deep water narrows to a ribbon, we found ourselves in the direct track of the great *Olympic*.

" Just where the wind *would* leave us, derelict like this, and just in mid-fairway," I said, rather uneasily ; and I tried to coax the yacht inshore.

FAWLEY BEACON, SOUTHAMPTON WATER

" The pilot up there on the bridge has got some searing words to loose off about us and our history, I bet," I added with something of a chuckle.

The liner was too near for comfort. The black hull bore down full upon us, and passed, towering like a black precipice of cliff. Close beside us—almost within arm's reach, it seemed—were the steel plates and rivets. Bugles sounded from somewhere in her deep interior. She was past.

The reappearance of the greatest liner traffic at Southampton has revived the port when it appeared to be faced with a period of decline. The port comes into its own yet once again after the many ups and downs ; changes of fortune have marked its whole history. First of all there was the Roman Clausentum on the Itchen when the site of Southampton itself was still a bare gravelly spit. The place, as it grew up, became the key of the rich Itchen valley, and Saxons and Danes time after time took it in their stride when they were aiming at richer plunder inland. Over and over again it was sacked and burnt.

Later, the Norman Conquest put a fresh face on everything. Regular traffic was set up with France, and Winchester had become the king's capital. Southampton lay in the direct line between Winchester and France, and naturally became a chief packet station. Then, with the decline of Winchester, Southampton declined also.

Sunshine to-day had now broken through the greyness ; we lay becalmed on oily water, broiled in heat.

" This would have put *all* the shipping on strike a hundred years ago," my companion said, as he heaved up a bucketful or two of water and sent them swashing along the thirsty decks. " Not a breath stirring."

True enough. Some of the earliest marine pictures of the English and Dutch schools show " shipping in a calm." The ships lie mirrored and inert. But Southampton-built ships were older by centuries than the old pictures. The ships of the Conqueror and the Plantagenet kings were here ; Henry II was a frequent passenger to and from Normandy, and Becket—left to look after things at home—used to meet him at Southampton on his return. The River Itchen had been made navigable to Alresford and Winchester, and Richard I saw that it was kept open for shipping. Henry V's fleets embarked troops here, and the same King (" Harry Fift ") founded at Southampton a storehouse and forge for his ships. *Holigost* was one of the King's ships, built here in 1414 ; she was followed by *Trinity Royal* (of 540 tons) in 1416.

It remained a great naval station, Portsmouth (a small place within its jurisdiction) being as yet insignificant. Until the reign of Henry VIII, indeed, Portsmouth was of small account ; but, once it began to develop, its rise was rapid ; and its rise brought decay to Southampton. In 1560 Southampton had already fallen away and was a declining port ; against the Armada it sent not one ship, and the Great Plague of 1665 seemed to give the *coup de grâce*. It was finished.

*Growler* hovered doubtfully, with little progress
to her credit, for four hours.   Four hours after we
had passed Calshot we had still failed to make good
our way to Fawley Beacon.   The decks were hot to
the touch.   These flat calms (as we had just been
saying) used to put their spell upon the old sailing
ships, but one is apt to forget the galleys.   The
flat calm was just the weather for them.   Galleys,
however, were never favoured greatly by our fore-
fathers in the Middle Ages, partly—it has been
conjectured — because   free   Englishmen   disliked
vessels so associated with slave labour.   Galleys
without number have nevertheless plied in Southampton Water ;   they were mostly foreigners, and
were often pirates.   In 1323 two Venetian galleys
—traders—were here ;   and galleys from Venice
continued to come for years with complete regularity.   From   1379,   for   a   period   of   150 years,
three to five galleys entered Southampton annually,
with merchandise from Genoa, Venice, Catalonia,
and Aragon.   In 1472, a regulation was made that
they must bring, as a proportion of their cargo,
bow-staves of Italian yew for our English archers.
Then Flanders galleys appeared in 1488, and certain
sturdy Englishmen ordered them—at their first
appearance—to strike sail.   The foreigners refused.
Knives were out at once, and men were killed on
both sides.   The Flemings—after reaching Southampton—sent a formal complaint to the King.
But the King refused to be drawn into these
trivial affairs of everyday homicide.   *De minimis
non curat lex*.   He sent word by the Bishop of

Winchester that " a pot of wine would settle the matter."

Of wine there should have been no lack at Southampton, for the port held at that time a

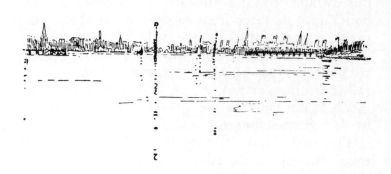

monopoly. No ship could discharge wine at any port in England without paying a duty to Southampton.

"Wake me at tea-time," my companion yawned;
"I'm dead sleepy in this sun."

Sunlight glistened upon the tidal flats, oozy and
bare, which lay beside us now that the tide was
down; the sun was westering and the afternoon had
come. A barge, becalmed astern of us, was imaged
in still water. Sunshine was bright upon the tier
of steamships at moorings beside Netley; the water
was unruffled. Its blue surface moved only with a
long, oily heave as the steamers went by.

But at last the breeze came, and *Growler* was away
for Southampton.

"This is better," I said as we rapidly made good
our distance towards the quays and floating dock.
Southampton water-front dispels visions of the past,
for it is modern to a degree; the eye gets a broad
impression of docks and quays on a great scale,
with cargo sheds on all hands, bonded warehouses,
railway sidings, cranes, sheers, grabs, and tips. And,
moored alongside as we passed, lay some of the
world's greatest liners.

The yacht was alive again. "A healthy contrast," my shipmate said, as he watched the foam
stream from us. Few contrasts are more inspiriting.
With sheets taut and sails drawing, *Growler* drove
through this blue water that was creased now and
furrowed with wind.

Up the Itchen for the moment we shaped our
course, beyond the floating ferry. It was as if we
could not sufficiently exploit our freedom; in our
inquisitive way—just like a terrier released from the
lead—we curved and doubled here and there.

· AT · ELING ·

The huge liners towered above us as we skirted the wharves back from the Itchen to Southampton town. Funnels and masts were everywhere, cropping up over warehouse roofs and railway stations.

The tide was high; but when—still sailing up Southampton Water—we left the town astern, we were careful to follow the channel all the same. I have seen more than one yacht go aground, once out of the fairway; and the margins of mud are broad. We sailed westward past Millbrook—again facing the New Forest.

" We can bring up here if the breeze fails. If the breeze holds, I vote we sail back and make the Hamble."

The fairway above Southampton was well marked, the booms on the starboard hand being surmounted by solid balls, those on port hand by cage balls. But everything will be different now, with the new docks beginning to come into the picture. Higher up, the channel divides, where the two shallow rivers—the Test and Bartley—enter. I have brought up for the night just below where they join, and have lain in great comfort there —outside all the bustle of Southampton; three miles above it, in point of fact. Eling has a quaint little water-front and is rather pleasant; but the river there dries out at low water, and the place is best approached by dinghy.

We were not bringing up here to-night. The breeze had not flattened at all, and the tide was turning seaward. The time was only seven o'clock; so we put *Growler* about, ran out the mainsheet, and romped back—full before the breeze. That golden sun was now astern of us as we again approached Southampton.

" Look at the men slung in cradles on the funnels of the *Aquitania*," my companion was pointing; " they're like Tom Thumbs or things out of *Gulliver's Travels*," he added. " Look at 'em."

We passed more rapidly this time. Down Southampton Water we sailed; the sun was now almost at point of setting, and Netley was losing the light.

" HOMERIC " AND " LEVIATHAN " AT SOUTHAMPTON

Evening had brought a greyer tone to all the landscape. We were soon off the mouth of the Hamble River; and, as we turned and shaped course north-eastward to pass between the two prominent booms that mark the approach to the river, we began to meet the Hamble ebb. Vigorous enough the current seemed as it bubbled by us; but the fair wind was sufficient, and it blew us smoothly in. The pier at Warsash slid by, and the " Crab and Lobster." Hamble village on the other bank was passed, and—in gathering twilight—we glided between the perches that lead through the marshes to Bursledon. Vikings and Saxons, Jutes and Danes have in their own day slipped quietly —like ourselves—between these marshes.

We had enjoyed it without comment, but now I broke silence :

" We want to get away with the ebb to-morrow. There's a nice little puff of wind now, and it may be flat calm then. Let's use it, and go back to Hamble to anchor instead of up here."

We agreed ; and, leaving Swanwick and Bursledon astern, we beat back in the last of the twilight.

Hamble River has history as ancient as that of Southampton Water ; with Southampton, too, it shared the reverse of fortune when naval activities were transferred from Southampton to Portsmouth. Hamble River was, in part, the cause of the transfer, for it had been the regular " lying-up " place for men-of-war. Leland referred to the creek as a place " wherein there is a fair road for great ships." And Portsmouth Dock, destined to change the whole face of affairs, was built when Henry VII's ships *Regent* and *Sovereign* were obviously too large for the Hamble.

But Hamble River did not at that period fall out of naval affairs so completely as did Southampton. It kept its shipbuilding. Between 1692 and 1695 Bursledon built three eighty-gun ships and one sixty ; in the following century it continued to build third- and fourth-rates. Splendid ghosts ought to haunt these waters. Bursledon was the birthplace of Nelson's seventy-four, the famous

VIKING SHIPS OF THE ANCIENT HAMBLE RIVER.

*Elephant.*  " Leave off action ?  Now damn me if
I do," said Nelson on her quarter-deck at Copenhagen.  And he put the telescope to the blind eye.
" I really do not see the signal ! " he exclaimed, and
presently :  " Damn  the  signal !  Keep  mine  for
closer battle flying !  That's the way I answer such
signals !  Nail mine to the mast ! "

At Copenhagen, too, attached to Riou's squadron,
was the frigate *Blanche*, built at Bursledon (1784).
Another frigate, more famous, was the *Penelope*, also
built here, in 1798.  Of thirty-six guns, that little
*Penelope*  engaged  the  eighty-gun  ship  *Guillaume
Tell* ;  and,  by  delaying  her  until  the  *Lion*  and
*Foudroyant* came up, secured her capture.  It was
a thing almost unknown for a frigate to attack a
ship of the line in this way.

The ebb had well-nigh uncovered the flats, and
had made plainer sailing for us, even in the half-
light.  Quietly we dropped with the ebb.

The congestion of moored yachts in row upon
row off Hamble looked denser.  It was a regular
city of masts beside the fairway ;  but the fairway
itself is open.  We had decided to anchor close to
the edge of the mud on the eastward side, taking our
chance of fouling one of the many chains and
anchors that encumber the ground.  The wind had
almost vanished, and the dark water was smooth as
glass when we came to anchor opposite Hamble.

The full name of the town is Hamble-le-Rice, and
Leland (in the reign of Henry VIII) called it " a
ood fisher town."  As already said, the creek was
" fair road  for  great ships."

Edward III, in 1375, ordered all ships of sixty tons or more from the south to assemble at Hamble, and Henry V was wont to have his fleet at anchor here when not on service. *Trinity Royal, Holigost, Grâce Dieu, Jesus,* and many another have lain where we were lying to-night, with the Hamble ebb and flow cluttering past their cables.

The night was very silent, and we lingered—pleased to be sequestered again from the world. The business of Southampton had quite faded out of the picture. Not a sound came to us in the darkness.

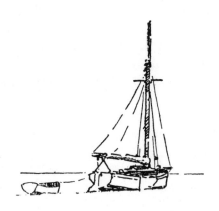

# CHAPTER X

## IN SANDOWN BAY

"SEA-FOG!" I called back over my shoulder into the cabin as I put my head out. Nothing was visible except white mist; Hamble village was nowhere, and moisture drip-dripped from our rigging. Hamble River was a sheet of glass.

"Nothing doing, then?" said my shipmate as he joined me in the well. "So we needn't hurry with breakfast."

We did not; but before we had washed up our crockery after the meal the sun was trying to shine through the mist, and we went ashore to explore Hamble. We climbed over those long stagings beside Luke's Yard. Sunlight was by this time bright in the village, but everything outside a hundred yards was still blotted and dim. The air was dead still.

We had been strolling between the thatched cottages, and I pulled up short as we reached the waterside again.

"Wind," I said. It was faint, but it was a real stirring in the air. "Let's get under way." And back to the dinghy we went.

As so often happens, the little touch of breeze had brought a thickening of the fog. But this did not trouble us, for the day was ours; minor incidents were possible, and the mud *might* capture us for a few hours, but with care—and the lead—we ought to be able to make good our escape. The light breeze was westerly, and we reached out, carried by the tide. We had no glimpse at all of Warsash as we passed it ; we were alone in fog.

Out somewhere there in the Solent was the booming of a liner's foghorn ; fog or no fog, the great shipping would be astir, and—when the limit of vision was little more than a few times the yacht's own length—we were keeping outside the main tracks of it. We shaped course for the shoal passage over the Brambles, sailing by compass from buoy to buoy ; when the Hamble buoy—dropping into the mist astern—had dimmed and evaporated, we were soon straining our eyes upon the grey curtain to find the Bald Head, and so on.

The great shipping still finds fog something of a nightmare ; it is a most unaccountable quantity, having tricks which are extraordinary. The man who is blind trusts more and more to his ears, and he is well advised to do so ; but not in fog. To the shipmaster, on days like this, the sense of sound is a treacherous guide. Fog often contains dead areas. You may hear some foghorn droning heavily to westward, and think you are well-nigh upon it ; but, sailing westward still, you lose the sound entirely, or hear it distantly as in a dream. The mariner must not, because he hears a foghorn faintly, think that he is at a great distance ; nor must he, because he hears the sound plainly, assume that he is near it. Definite advice to that effect is tendered in the Admiralty directions. When closing the land in fog the lead is the only safe guide, unless at points where the submarine bell is used. The submarine bell is wholly unaffected by the dead areas of a fog.

Our own science to-day, as we left the Hamble, was primitive. *Growler's* course was by compass only, for the slight cross-drift of tide could be safely neglected. The light breeze remained steady, and the buoys took vague shape and materialised swiftly —right over the bowsprit every time. There was no glimpse of Calshot Castle, but we must find Calshot Float, and, after it, the Hill Head buoy and the East Brambles.

Look-out was strict and careful. We heard the flat-flat-flat sound of paddle wheels, and almost instantly an excursion steamer had sprung from the mist, straight upon us.

" She's laying course—like us—from buoy to buoy, and ticking 'em off, one by one, all the way up Southampton Water."

She vanished into the grey. Another steamer followed closely in her wake, springing upon us in just the same fashion, out of the fog.

But sometimes—strain our eyes as we would—we heard only, and saw nothing. The ball of the sun was now again visible ; it became a golden blot above, but the mist on the water was thick as ever, and the look-out to sunward was tiring to the eyes ; one blinked and blinked. The sound of the engine of a motor-boat could be heard, but the boat was nowhere ; there were voices of men, so clear that every word could be caught—but the boat went by invisibly; we strained our eyes, and there was never a glimpse. Without showing us the thinnest vestige of shape the boat was gone.

Somewhere in the mist over there lay Titchfield Haven. This haven dries at low water, but it possesses a little tongue of land—a very little one—which gives shelter to a moored vessel at high water. This shelter is welcome, as the place is a lee shore in south-westerly winds. Shoreward, the immediate background is pleasant, with an inland sheet of water, reed-bordered, and quiet lanes.

Then, off Stokes Bay, the broad seascape opened as by magic, and the sun was shining upon a rippled blue sea. The fog had held until half-past twelve, but it had gone decisively now, and the wind had really come to life.

Round Bembridge Ledge, a mile off this low coastland, we sailed, inshore of the Nab Rock and the Princessa shoal. And there, over the bowsprit, was the great cliff of Culver, building itself higher and higher as we closed the shore of White Cliff Bay. With her light draught *Growler* could sail shoreward until the sunlit precipice overhung us, ivory-white against the blue.

Crannied and flint-scarred, it breaks perpendicularly to the sea. It beetled now above us, inhabited —here and there—by rock-pigeons and ravens. We could hear the cawing of the ravens; the sound was almost sepulchral among the rock-faces. A shadow drifted over the sun, and there was an eerie quality in the solitude, beside this inaccessible chalk.

With long leg and short we sailed close-hauled

for Shanklin ; the headland of Dunnose was beyond. Crossing the bay, we sailed towards its dark outline, so great a contrast—heavy-coloured, and in shadow under the sun—to the sunlit grace of Culver.

At Dunnose is the beginning of St. Catherine's Race, which is apt to be an uncomfortable stretch of

SHANKLIN, SANDOWN, AND CULVER CLIFF

water, even in calm weather. But we should not encounter it to-day ; had I indeed been really out-ward bound I should have made a good offing from the shore, and kept right outside.

Shanklin and Sandown lie beside one another, each

with its own pier ; and the foreshore to-day was a chequer-work of colour, with the crowds on holiday. Off Shanklin pier we let go our anchor.

When I want to go for a real ramble, I prefer to leave the yacht snugly moored at Bembridge, out of harm's way, whatever may happen. I can then stretch my legs ashore with a mind really at rest.

Old Shanklin church was founded in the early fourteenth century ; a path leads from the church-yard (reached by stone steps over the churchyard wall) to the downs. Or, by the cliff paths, you can strike out towards Luccombe. On these cliffs, especially in the twilight, the isolation is still complete. One can fancy the old French fleets that anchored in the bay in 1545, or the French priva-teers that sailed up this coast little more than a hundred years ago. The open landscape is un-changed.

Our pause was short to-day ; we were away almost at once. Our wind free, we sailed past Sandown, close inshore. Sandown, once held by Ulnod the Saxon, figures in the *Domesday Book* of 1086 as " Sande." Then, for some centuries, little is heard of it, until Henry VIII built the castle, as part of his general scheme of defence of the Island. Record remains that the first Captain of " Sandam Castle " was wont to attend Arreton Church in a " wrought velvet gowne," twelve sol-diers with halberds marching as his bodyguard. The castle was entirely rebuilt by Charles I.

Culver Cliff was now again over the bows, and again we rounded it, close inshore. This bay which we were leaving—Sandown Bay—was, like the road off St. Helens, a regular anchorage in its day. John Wilkes, in 1778, said he had twice counted 150 ships, principally merchantmen, at anchor.

" Peaceful, this," I said, as I looked up at the white chalk and down at the blue sea around us.

A long swell set us rolling as we moved serenely northward, dropping Culver gradually astern. Then, as we made good our way to the Bembridge Ledges, the wind fell away, leaving us almost becalmed. And the sunlight vanished, for the banks of mist had again rolled over the downs ; the coastline was gone.

" Rather a bore if we can't get into harbour," said my shipmate.

" Yes," I answered. " You can sit in the well and ring the fog-bell all night ! "

We rolled and rocked in the grey swell, blanketed in fog. It really seemed as if, through lack of wind, we should be unable to reach Bembridge ; but light airs still came in very small puffs, and we maintained gradual headway, closing the shore and searching for the Drumhead buoy through the grey curtain. The fog curdled up from the water about us, densely ; it was eddying with the breeze. We could anchor outside, if need be, but the sense of a harbour about us would give us a better night's sleep.

" St. Helens Fort ! "

We were glad, in the shadowy dusk, to have stumbled on it ; there in the mist it was, sure enough, and we were just on course. The lead had shown

THE OLD COTTAGES AT SHANKLIN

that we were keeping near the edge of the sand. The shape of the Drumhead buoy was next dimly discovered. We were soon in harbour, and the fog grew denser in the nightfall. Moored with the shore close aboard us though we were, nothing at all was visible. There was nothing but fog. We were glad to be in.

# CHAPTER XI

## SPITHEAD

ON a dull evening which was dark and quite forbidding we left Bembridge again. The wind, southerly, was bringing up a lop of sea outside—nothing important, but enough to make the yacht lively. We were soon at sea, and we reached right away for Chichester Harbour, making, in the half-light, as salt a little sea passage as one could wish. At high water, the steep waves on the bar at Chichester were no danger, though they were breaking freely with this wind as we fetched them astern and ran free through the broad entrance. Immediately inside, we brought up off Hayling Island, at Sandy Point, in Mengham Rithe. Shelter was entire, though a slight roll was felt from the open sea so near at hand. It is an excellent anchorage, with the pebbly beach close aboard.

Departure from Chichester was under conditions widely different. Morning was windless, with a blue sky. The ebb-tide sucked the yacht out seaward as soon as the anchor left the ground ; smoothly past the yellow shingle she glided. With a light breeze, which she picked up outside, she was able to make good some distance against the tidal current towards the Isle of Wight (which lay there on the near horizon, looking so like an Isle of Promise, as it always does) ; but then again the breeze deserted her and she drifted.

A better air began to pipe after midday, so that we were able to bring the Nomansland Fort abeam, thus entering Spithead. The sight of roadsteads, empty now, which once teemed with shipping is a sight which always has a certain appeal to the imagination ; and Spithead is a notable example The natural advantages for the assembling of fleets were so obvious that the roadstead was used by every generation ; and, in the latter days of sail, the tall fleets must have been a splendid picture.

The earliest history of Spithead is lost in the far past ; but we hear of the roadstead in A.D. 296, when the fleet of Allectus was anchored here. Fleet after fleet followed, type after type, rig after rig.

The Jutes and Saxons who displaced the Romans from the Isle of Wight possibly preferred the inlets and havens for their long-boats, and the Danes who harried them in turn probably did the same. The Danish pirates used the island as a base, and " lived at discretion, no force being able to withstand them." Then, in course of years, came the threat to England from Normandy, and Harold assembled a great fleet here to resist the coming of William. Unfortunately for him, he allowed it gradually to disperse, and William landed at Pevensey, unopposed.

Our wind to-day breezed up from the west, and we were beating towards Stokes Bay (Stocke Bay in its old years). Wind and tide were against us, and we made slow progress ; but we really had no fixed objective to windward, and were content with sea and sunshine.

King John assembled a fleet at Portsmouth and Spithead in 1205, for an expedition to France which, in fact, proved abortive. Then commercial activity developed as years went on, so that covetous eyes began to watch the rich cargoes that were passing to and fro. In the reign of Henry IV gangs of desperadoes from Portsmouth used to frequent these waters and to terrorise shipping; and a century later the grip of the pirates was so close that it was strangling the very life of Southampton.

In the reigns of Henry VII and VIII England began to reassert her position as a maritime power. Henry VII built great ocean-carriers, and Henry VIII built battleships. The ships of the latter King were designed for war, and for war only. When, in 1544, the French were in force off St. Helens, the *Henry Grâce à Dieu* was in action, and the good ship *Mary Rose* was also in the fleet which sailed to repel the incursion. The *Mary Rose* was one of Henry's favourites. He had just himself dined aboard her; she was described as " the flower of all ships that ever sailed." Henry, shrewd beyond his generation, had foreseen how weight of metal would be the foremost factor in determining battles, and he armed his ships accordingly with the largest guns which he could obtain. Perhaps the weight of her ordnance had made the *Mary Rose* top-heavy and crank; at all events, her gun-ports, which were less than two feet above the water-line, had been left open, and—in a sudden squall—she heeled and capsised. With her captain, Sir George Carew, and her whole crew of 400 men, she sank.

The Venetians, who were early experts in salvage, made efforts to raise her, but without success.

A like tragedy (made famous to all generations by Cowper's poem) occurred more than two centuries later, in 1782—the loss of the *Royal George*. The *Royal George* carried the highest masts of any ship in the British Navy, and her metal was the heaviest. She had seen twenty-six years' service, always as a flagship. She had carried the flags of Hawke, Boscawen, Rodney, Howe, Kempenfelt; she was Hawke's flagship at Quiberon Bay. But she had been neglected shamefully; her timbers were decayed and unrenewed; in boat-builders' phrase, she was "ripe as a pear." There was no squall; *pace* Cowper, no "land-breeze shook the shrouds." At the moment, she was being careened for repairs, and her side fairly broke away from her, ripped away with an awful rending, and down she went in a moment. Kempenfelt, pen in hand in the admiral's cabin, went down "with twice four hundred men."

It is chiefly through Cowper's poem, and his own tragic death, that Kempenfelt is known to posterity. But he deserves a fame of quite a different order. Not only a fighting admiral, he was a student and thinker. He had seen that the time-honoured method of signalling, by means of attaching a certain significance to specified flags, was inadequate; upon occasions it had led to grotesque misunderstandings. In 1782, the year of his death, he had

THE GOOD SHIP " MARY ROSE "

produced his *Primer of Speech for Fighting Ships* which was the Navy's first "Signal Book." It enabled (by means of its phrase-book with numbered words) any message to be signalled with precision; the admiral could speak to any vessel, or to his whole fleet, as he wished. It was Kempenfelt's signal book which enabled Nelson to signal to his fleet at Trafalgar that "England expects that every man will do his duty."

That young seaman in the merchant service, Samuel Kelly (a young sailor whose memoirs were recently discovered and published), arrived in Spithead from America just after the *Royal George* had sunk. He says:

"On running down to the Mother Bank, we passed a ship sunk, which was found to be the *Royal George* (a first Rate). . . . After we anchored, our captain went on shore to Portsmouth and ordered a new cable. Whilst we were waiting for this, the dead bodies belonging to the *Royal George* floated and passed our ship both with ebb and flood tide; many we perceived on the shore at low water, and some I saw fastened by ropes to the buoy of a ship at Spithead."

The masts of the wreck were above water, and a large capstan-hoy was fast to them, from which diving-bells were being worked. Young Kelly more than once went to watch it, "Keeping a good look-out that I did not get the boatswain's supplejack on my back," he says. For he was, of course, a trespasser on the hoy, which was "crowded with

AT SOUTHAMPTON

A FAIR WIND OFF CULVER CLIFF

naval officers from the fleet at Spithead "; but there were many hangers-on present. Once—being mistaken for a regular member of the crew—Kelly found himself " driven to the capstans."

The rigging of the *Royal George* was decorated, he says, " not with colours, but with dead bodies, which presented a horrid spectacle." The bodies had floated at high water, and had been secured to the shrouds and mainstays to prevent the tide from carrying them away. At low tide they hung there, several feet above the water.

A roadstead which was so long the anchorage of great fleets is bound to have a long history of minor happenings. There were accidents, for instance, such as the destruction by fire of H.M.S. *Boyne*, a ninety-eight-gun ship, in 1795. With fire issuing from every porthole, she drifted right into Portsmouth Harbour, a lurid picture ; her guns, as it happened, were shotted, and they fired themselves one after another as she drove in, causing damage everywhere. Finally, the flames reached her magazine and she blew up.

Amazingly picturesque the roadstead must have been with the tall fleets at anchor or making sail. From Spithead they sailed for the wars, trim and stately, and they returned to it again shot-battered, with their battle-scars and their prizes. Spithead was occupied by Blake's ships in the days of the Parliament ; then the fleets of Torrington, Anson, and Hawke lay successively in the roadstead. Wolfe's expedition to North America was fitted out at Portsmouth, and the dead general was brought back here, his body being landed at Portsmouth, to the sound of minute guns from the fleet at Spithead.

Ships just returned from long commissions were always a great contrast to the sprucely painted Home Fleet. The weather-worn vessel would be surrounded with " Jews and women " almost before she had come to anchor. Discipline for the while was relaxed ; a first-rate (Mr. Masefield tells us) might have as many as 500 women aboard at the same time. Drink—despite every precaution—was smuggled on board, and the sailors and women " drank and quarrelled among the guns."

The ordinary routine presents a more attractive picture—a picture of perfect order and cleanliness. The fleets were cities afloat, with their ordered round of work, and the hum of men crowded between the wooden walls. Spotless and burnished they lay—the smell of hemp and paint about them. In the dawn the barelegged men would be washing down the decks ; then with sprinkled sand and holystone they would make them spotless white. All brasswork would be made to shine like beaten gold. And so—from duty to duty—the day's work would be carried through.

But the placid routine was not always running smoothly. A tag of familiar rhyme (attributed by some to Quarles) has it thus :

> God and the sailor we alike adore,
> But only when in danger, not before ;
> The danger o'er, both are alike requited,
> God is forgotten and the sailor slighted.

THE LINER

The nation in peace-time has always been apt to forget the Navy; and in the reign of Charles I, when Buckingham's expedition to Spain was fitted out, the flagship was the old *Ark Royal*, which had fought the Armada forty years before, and some ships were even wearing the same sails as they had in that year. The crews were equally neglected; food was bad and pay uncertain. The whole fleet was in a state of sickness and mutiny. But Buckingham was not the man to share the hardships of the fleet; he held himself completely aloof, having reserved to himself a special transport and kitchen.

Under the Commonwealth everything was changed, and the Navy was really given due regard; more than half the annual revenue was spent upon it, and Blake—who believed in having a happy lower deck—saw that good pay was given. But the change hardly outlived the Restoration; pay again became uncertain and conditions wretched.

As years went on, moreover, the ships were filled with pressed men—men who had been earning good money elsewhere, and had no wish to be thrust under the grim discipline of the Navy, with bad food and uncertain pay.

Things came to a head in 1797. The sailors seem clearly to have been anxious to submit their grievances, in an orderly and respectful manner, to the authorities. But the Government was both dilatory and unsympathetic, and the mutiny at Spithead resulted—with scenes of bloodshed and violence. Lord Howe, the victor of the Glorious First of June, was appointed to settle matters, and

was given powers little short of absolute. Trusted
as he was throughout the fleet, he effected a settlement based upon reason and not upon coercion,
feeling no doubt that the sailors, though wrong,
had been greatly wronged also.

This period—the close of the eighteenth century
—was one in which smuggling was rife, here as
elsewhere. And the smugglers were used by the
Intelligence Departments of the Fighting Services
during the Napoleonic Wars. With their secret
flittings from coast to coast they could obtain infor-
mation which was otherwise difficult to come by.
The smugglers helped both sides; but in point of
fact the French were better served by them than
we were. Movements of vessels in Spithead, and
in and out of the south coast ports, were known to
these free-traders, and could be reported to the other
side, whereas arrivals of French ships in the Bay of
Biscay were outside the natural radius of the
smugglers' traffic.

. . . . . .

The coastwise tide to-day had now turned in our
favour, but the breeze which had sprung up was
heading us. It was slow work.

Gradually, however, the tide helping her, the
yacht made good her passage westward. One long
tack carried her across to the East Brambles buoy,
opposite Lee-on-the-Solent. The buoy is one of
those marking the great patch of shoal which prevents
direct entrance to Southampton Water along the
eastward side.

"We shan't see Yarmouth to-day," my shipmate commented, as he looked across the broad water that was all too smooth and lake-like ; but there was no touch of disappointment in his tone. Wind for a real passage was lacking. We slid pleasantly through the water ; more and more slowly we sailed, but it did not matter in the least. The evening—now almost upon us—was one of perfect

A SEVENTY-FOUR

contentment, and — after all — "to-morrow is another day." It is the oriental view ; and the yachtsman, dependent, like primitive man, upon the direct mood of Nature, is apt to develop a like fatalism. "What will be, will be."

Through Spithead we had turned, once forested with tall spars ; it was empty. Across to the Island

again, we made good our passage to Old Castle
Point at East Cowes ; but the friendly tide was
finished, and—feeling inclined for an anchorage
more sequestered than that of Cowes—we put up
the helm, and slipped eastward again before the
dying wind, past Norris Castle to the wooded slopes
of Osborne. Then, in the very last of the low
sunlight, we let go our anchor close inshore. The
wind died with the sunlight, leaving a flat calm.

In the twilight we lingered on deck. The yacht
was not dead-still, for a slight roll from the sea outside kept her lightly aswing. It was a perfect evening.

.    .    .    .    .    .

Spithead is lake-like when in quiet mood. But,
with a strong breeze, it becomes quite an awkward
seaway for smaller craft ; its waves are much more
disconcerting to a small yacht than the seas outside,
which—though so very much larger—are less steep
and sudden. A few days later we were again
turning to windward, bound this time for Beaulieu
River, through a dirty seaway. The yacht tumbled
about and *smacked* the seas, and *thudded* against
them. The spray flew. This had been all very
well as long as the tide was with us, for we made
solid progress all the time. But the tide was now
contrary ; and, with a yacht of barge type, the
thing was a struggle. If heed were relaxed in the
least we should merely turn offshore and onshore
again, without profit, perhaps managing to maintain
her position, perhaps being sucked beamwise back.
We were skirting the mainland, and the only chance

was to cheat the tide by sailing in the shoalest water. On the shoreward board, therefore, one of us kept his hand on the chain of the lee-board, and the moment the chain slacked the least atom, showing that the board had touched, he shouted, " Lee ho ! " The automatic sounding device ensured that she should sail to the utmost limit in shallow water. It answered perfectly, but the thing was a long struggle. We entered the river obliquely over anything that would float us, shying off seaward a little if the board lifted, and then sneaking in again. This was the only way ; and we could take no harm—for the tide was making. Once in the river, we soon beat up to Needs Oar, reached on to Gilbury, and then beat to Bucklers Hard in the last of the light. The clouds parted now and again after we had anchored, and gave us fleeting gleams of moonlight.

# CHAPTER XII

## ABOUT POOLE HARBOUR

" SUNSHINE ! "

We stirred willingly from our bunks and turned out. A splendid morning, this, with a brisk north-westerly wind. We had to go up to Beaulieu for provisions ; so the sail of the dinghy was set, and away we went. Shadow and shine chased each other over the New Forest landscape, and we wound our way, between the rushy borders, to Beaulieu.

Back again with the ebb, we were on board by afternoon and were making sail in earnest. The tide was too low to admit of escape by way of Bull-lake ; we must therefore sail the full distance down to Lepe, and back again (in the Solent) on the other side of the long mud flat. It took us an hour and a quarter to sail from Needs Oar back to Needs Oar, via Lepe, hairpin fashion.

Outside, the Solent tide was against us, but we made good our way over it, though slowly. The afternoon was perfect, and the whole thing was a perfection of indolent sailing. We could just lay our course ; and the distant downs began gradually to rise on the skyline to southward, behind the earth cliffs of the Island. Newtown River was passed, some miles distant, and Bouldnor Cliff. Then the downs rose again, beyond the cliff, and

PAST THE LIGHTHOUSE AT
HURST CASTLE

so on, until we were abreast of the Lymington Banks buoy, and the Needles were opened clear of the land. The time was now half-past seven, and evening was drawing on. On the Island side, Yarmouth town, with its little square church tower, was abeam, and there beside us was Jack-in-the-Basket.

Half an hour later we were beside that long shingle-bank of Hurst Castle.

"The tide ought to be just on the turn; I think we've timed it pretty correctly. We shouldn't get through the North Channel at all to-night against the tide."

The tide is rather a complex affair. When one is bound for the North Channel and the wind is light it is necessary to jockey for position, and

to get carried by the right stream.    The ebb splits
about a third of the way across between Hurst and
Cliff End, one part setting fairly through the North
Channel, and the other south of the Shingles shoal,
and across it, to the Needles.    Also, as the *Channel
Pilot* says : " A strong eddy which runs between the
junction of the tides and the point [Hurst] must be
carefully avoided, for, in it, a sailing vessel becomes
totally unmanageable."

There were two lions in the path—the Shingles
and that eddy.    The stream would suck us towards
the Shingles.

The eddy, moreover, sounds distinctly unpleasant
in the Admiralty description, and it has more than
once been a minor anxiety in very light airs.    When
the breeze is good the passage can of course be
negotiated with decision.

The breeze this evening was not a strong one,
and it would head us through the channel.    With
a fair wind, one keeps the shingle-bank close aboard,
and romps through without touching the broken
water at all.    But to-day we should have to beat.
We had steered close to the Point, but were set off
beamwise at once ;  and we were soon in the broken
water.    The tiller was wrenched this way and that,
and the yacht was only half-compliant ;  a stronger
breeze would have been welcome here, even if it
had knocked up a real tumble of sea.    We watched
the Shingles buoy critically, for in that direction—
of all places—we must not allow ourselves to be
drawn ;  inshore and offshore, we made short boards
and worked through the Channel.    Hurst Castle,

with each tack, jutted out farther and farther astern of us, covering Sconce Point ; we were through the narrow gut now, and our attention could again relax.

" That's that." We were fairly at sea, and glad to be there.

Busy as we had been turning to windward, we had scarcely noticed the nightfall, but night was now really upon us. There was a sunset, already deadening, over Milford and Hengistbury Head, and the great moon had risen astern of us. We settled down to full enjoyment of it all, top-coated now, for the night had become chill. The sea was less smooth than might have been expected ; the waves threw us about as we turned to windward over them. Under the moon was the path of tumbling silver glitter ; and far away astern of us the chalk cliff of the Island, touched with moonlight, stood up, phantom-white.

The wind was more westerly and was breezing up. Lights now glittered into life here and there ; the fort of Hurst had dropped below the shingle-bank, but the beam of the lighthouse was bright above it ; the Needles light was red, away there astern of us, and a bevy of twinkling pin-points showed where Milford lay on the mainland shore on the starboard hand. We thrashed on.

It was odd to step from the cold night into the cabin ; the warmth of the day's sunshine still lingered there. The very smell of the hot sunshine on Beaulieu woodlands and the smooth Solent had been carried with us out here, where a cold lumpy seaway was about us, furrowed with a night breeze.

" We're getting on. We've obscured Hurst and turned the Needles from red to white."

" Yes," my companion assented, " and we've raised Anvil."

So we had. Away to westward, Anvil light (beyond Swanage) was clear enough, and the flashes from St. Catherine's far astern of us, were also visible as the beam wheeled round the sky ; but the light itself was below the horizon.

Before midnight we had hauled Hengistbury Head abeam, behind which is the narrow entrance to Christchurch Harbour. The bar is apt to change with every storm, and the local men alone can be trusted for the latest details ; it is useless to trust to pilot books. Not only the position of the entrance varies ; its depth varies also. Thus a vessel drawing seven feet of water might successfully enter, but a day or two later—after a storm—she might find herself locked in, so to speak, unable to escape. The harbour is a delightful place for exploration in a small boat ; and Hengistbury Head is a breezy foreland from which a view of the whole harbour is gained. Turning about, one commands miles of blue sea, with the Isle of Wight on the skyline.

" I can just make out the shape of Hengistbury Head. See the loom of it there ? " I pointed into the darkness. " It's barely distinguishable to-night, a couple of miles off."

The yacht plunged and thrashed ; she threw up sheets of spray which hid the horizon as she dipped, and then her bows shot upward into the sky again. The tiller was kicking, hard.

On a shoreward board, we were next able to make out the red light on Boscombe Pier. Bournemouth stretched beyond it in the night.

" We ought to be able to see the fairway buoy for Poole ; it's lighted." I scanned the darkness towards Studland Bay, but the light seemed inordinately long in twinkling up on the broken sealine. To and fro in the night, on and off, through the dark seaway we sailed, board after board.

" There it is, surely."

By its bearing the direction was right enough, and the flashing pin-prick was certainly there. I climbed from the well, and clung to the shrouds, watching, while the dark water churned and gurgled away, washing noisily, and the spray flew about me. No, the light had gone.

We thrashed on for half an hour longer, and I again hoisted myself up to look out. Yes, there it was ; invisible from the well, it was clear enough from here ; it *was* the buoy. But why, half an hour before, it should have made itself visible even from the well, and should then have disappeared *completely*, I do not know. Possibly a series of larger waves than usual had just brought it up higher at that moment.

The fixed lights at Poole entrance were clear enough, and they seemed to mock at our slow progress. Wide apart they hung, and we seemed simply unable to close them up and bring them into line.

AT·DAWN.

"I want to turn in," my shipmate yawned. "I want to get there; this is slow."

"Yes," I answered, both hands on the tiller as it kicked; "yes, and we won't bother to make Poole this tide; we'll let go in Studland and have a nap."

Lights could be seen in Swanage now, and we had closed up the headlands so that Anvil light was lost. We were getting on. Then the first gleam of dawn stole into the sky to eastward, and the moon was setting goldenly over Durlstone (by Swanage). Nearer, nearer, at last—here was the buoy, and we seemed sailing swiftly enough as we passed it.

A tramp steamer lay anchored near the buoy; she had been vague in the dusk to windward, and was now bold against the dawn when we had passed her. I went below for something, and, as I emerged, my companion's dark figure against the dawn was in silhouette. Dew was on the cabin-top, and the breeze was freshening as the light broadened.

A rose-red flush was over everything as we neared the shelter of the white cliffs of Studland, and the water had become smooth under the lee of the land. Close in to the Old Harry Rocks we stood before going about, and the seagulls were clanging in chorus about the deserted cliffs. A lonely world it was, in the half-light, all steeped in the pink glow. There was a strangeness about it all, a primitive quality. This was a fit setting for Alfred's first sea-fight against the Danes, which occurred off these very rocks. Up into the bay we steered, close inshore, but clear of the rocks off the Red Cliff; and there, by the lead, we brought up. Down went the anchor, and the sails were furled in quick time. Nothing hindered now, and we were below and fast asleep in the space of minutes.

.        .        .        .        .        .

We slept, I suppose, until midday. Then we turned out, in a wonder-world of sunlight, to a picture of white cliffs and smooth blue sea. We yawned, with a full sense of indolence and well-being, and we sat down on the cabin-top in complete contentment.

This was too supremely good to be bartered for any other anchorage just now. We could not go back into bonds again, even to the extent of entering a landlocked harbour.

The breeze came pleasantly from the shore, with a smell of sun-warmed turf, and it crisped the blue surface as it came.

When we had fed and cleared up, the afternoon was well upon us.

" I feel like a stretch ashore," one of us said, eyeing those smooth-turfed downs.

Agreed. We pulled ashore in the dinghy; and then, through the trees, and past the old stone cottages, thatch-roofed, we gained the open cliff-top. On Ballard Down we sprawled in the sun-shine.

We did not drowse; but we had no wish to talk —simply to laze was enough, looking seaward. Sheep browsed on the lower slopes and an occasional butterfly flitted by us out of the gorse bushes.

We retraced our path to the shore with slow steps as the sun westered. The beach was deserted, save by a few fishermen; and evening was warm and pleasant.

" Won't be so warm, not to-morrow, I dare say," one of the fishermen said, as I gave him a hand with his boat, which he was dragging up the sandy beach.

One's eye instinctively scanned the horizon for some sign of change. The old-fashioned shellback-oracles were so swift to divine these things. But this fisherman dispelled the halo. "Forecast says fresh northerly winds," he added, and then, "We'll see what the wireless says to-night," he finished. *Tempora mutantur !*

Back on board we pulled.

"North wind, eh ? " I said. "A blow from the nor'-east would catch us a little close to the lee shore for getting away." Rather grudgingly we made sail, and anchored somewhat farther offshore before we turned in.

. . . . .

Before daylight I was conscious of *noise*. The wind had breezed up in the night ; it was nothing much, but enough to make us take on a strong roll, and to start all the hundred and one noises that come from somewhere. The lee-boards clattered and the cable ground on the bobstay.

"Keep you awake ? " I asked my drowsy ship-mate, as he blinked into wakefulness in the morning in a very unstable cabin.

"Not a bit," he yawned. "Honest ship-noises."

Studland had lost its merit as an anchorage, and we made sail and entered Poole Harbour. It is a wonderful inland haven, entered by a narrow sound, through which the tide sluices pretty fast at Springs. The chain-ferry is now installed, but there was no

OLD HARRY ROCKS

chain-ferry then.   In we sailed between Sandbanks
and South Haven Point, and were soon in smooth
water.

"*Pool*," wrote Grenville Collins in 1692, " is a
Bar-Haven and lyeth five Leagues to the westward
of the *Needles*, or *Isle of Wight*, where Ships sail in
with a High-tyde.   I have not as yet survey'd *Pool*
Harbour, but 'tis intended, God willing."

The harbour has since been accurately surveyed
and beaconed and buoyed, so that the main channel
(sweeping round in a long curve) to Poole is easily
followed by day or night.   But the marking of the
minor channels is not always so easily followed, and
we did a little unintentional surveying on our own
account now and again.

That same evening, for instance, we determined
to lie in Wych Channel, west of Brownsea Island,
where shelter from the north-east wind would be
complete.   The beacons, lavish on the chart, were
remarkably few in reality.   But a barge yacht, if
carefully handled, can take far more chances in the
mud-game than other craft ;   her lee-boards, if
watched, give her ample warning.

In a grey evening we let go our anchor.   Brownsea
Island, a dark silhouette of steep land crowned with
ragged fir-trees, was close aboard.

The change from Studland was entire—in sur-
roundings, in atmosphere, and in quality.   Save
for the steepness of Brownsea cliffs we might be
back among the estuaries of the east coast.   The
wind had taken off again, and the sullen grey water
fell smooth.   The water was turbid, a contrast to

the green limpidity of the sea at Studland, through which the rocks and sand were visible, through fifteen feet of water.

This harbour was a great place for smugglers of old time.   The genial picture of

> Five and twenty ponies,
> Trotting through the dark—
> Brandy for the Parson,
> 'Baccy for the Clerk,

leaves the impression of a good-natured, if nefarious, trade.   In point of fact, the south of England smugglers of the mid-eighteenth century perpetrated "peculiarly revolting deeds that have in them nothing of romance ; nothing but a long-drawn story of villainy and fiendish cruelty."   Cold-blooded murders were perpetual, and dwellers in solitary situations were kept in a state of terror. The cruelties were almost beyond belief.

Until a century ago both smuggler and pirate were still in being.   The pirate also has his halo in romantic literature ; he also was less congenial in cold fact.   As an instance, one of the Western Ocean packets, a passenger vessel diverted to a Calcutta voyage, was captured by pirates on the high seas as late as 1829, and every one on board was butchered.

Some centuries before, round about the year 1400, Poole had a famous local pirate of its own. One Harry Page, a bold Poole mariner, made himself a terror to French and Spanish merchantmen.   To his victims Harry Page went by the name of " Arri-pay."   He is said on one occasion to have brought as many as 120 prizes home to Poole.

So here was Poole Harbour, with its wide distances and winding creeks. Sailing in the yacht, or twisting up narrower channels in the dinghy, I have—at one time or another—explored the corners and islands of the harbour with some completeness.

The very next morning, for instance, we were away to Shipstal Point. The amenities of Poole Harbour are distinctly prejudiced by notice-boards—it is a place where reasonable access to some part of the islands and other foreshores might be expected. Even at Shipstal Point the " wooden falsehood " is in evidence : " Trespassers will be prosecuted." As trespass, apart from wilful damage, is no offence, prosecution is impossible—the remedy being a civil one. " The Police have strict orders," etc., is an even more flagrant misstatement, but both are still freely indulged by the landowners. The civil authorities at Poole have taken the matter up, not in regard to these unlawful threats, but in regard to the unlawful attempts at private encroachment. They now " beat the bounds " of the harbour, and see that public rights of access are not further curtailed.

Landing at Shipstal Point, beside the small cottages, we half expected a hostile reception, especially as all the population, including the dogs, turned out in force. Putting a bold face on it, we tramped up the track to the heathered uplands. No one said us nay, and it appeared, on inquiry, that the spot was one to which the Corporation of Poole had made good the right of the public. We went far enough to get a view of the harbour outspread, and then returned to the dinghy.

IN POOLE HARBOUR
(CREECH BARROW IN THE DISTANCE)

We sailed back south of Long Island and Round Island, both of which are private.

Another day we anchored off Goathorn Point, where good shelter from south-westerly winds is obtained. From that anchorage we explored Furzey Island and Green Island, where the usual *verbotens* are in evidence. Approaching in the dinghy, I have sometimes been warned off from such places, though not from these particular islands.

" No landing here ! " is shouted. Perhaps I am intending to sketch from the shore, and the dinghy is still pulled manfully in.

" Don't you hear ?  No landing !  Private property," come the rasping words, repeated in a shout.

The dinghy still heads shoreward, and my interlocutor is hopping, like a pea in a shovel, about the water's edge.

" Are you deaf ? " etc., etc., etc.

For answer, I splash, sea-booted, into the shallow water and pull the dinghy up.  " No one on God's earth," I assure my enemy coldly, " can prevent me from landing below high-water mark."  And there I stop, and carry on with my own lawful occasions.

We landed one evening at Furzey, where the whole world was a solitude.  Taking care not to cross high-water mark, we paced along the shore.  Beside a little pier, we saw the inevitable notice-board ; its back was turned towards us, but we made our guesses as to the words we should find upon it. Humour is defined as a " nice perception of the incongruous " ; and, if so, my own shot perhaps earned the honest laughter which my shipmate gave it. " Minerals," I said.

Seen in plan from Swanage Downs, Poole Harbour looks a delightful place for romance and discovery. Actually it is a rather sad commentary upon human nature. The notice-boards have no doubt been brought into being largely because a vandal public insists on leaving a trail of litter and destruction.

That night we lay at anchor off Goathorn Point, close to the little pier at which stone was being loaded into barges for the training wall at the harbour entrance. The moon was at the full. Loitering on deck long after my shipmate had turned in, I was alone. A light breeze rippled the water, and the woody slopes and heathered distances were about us on every hand. The moon-track was golden in the water.

Goathorn Quay has been a regular landing-place for the smugglers' runs in its time ; it is primitive and isolated still—out of the world.

Sandbanks, just inside the harbour entrance, was equally unfrequented a few years ago. But the sandhills are now built over, and the place has become an outlying suburb of Bournemouth. Off Sandbanks, *Growler* has been moored more often than at any place in Poole Harbour (saving Poole itself, where she was laid up one winter) ; and next morning she shifted across to Sandbanks. With a brisk south-westerly wind, a jib was all that was needed. She skimmed rapidly down South Deep and across the harbour entrance, getting one glimpse of the sea outside. Then, meeting the ebb from

North Haven Lake, her speed was checked; and the one sail was furled just in time to bring her up, dead still, on a mooring buoy.

Easily accessible from town, Sandbanks became my base for best part of one summer season. Returning to the yacht some evening there, one can find Poole Harbour a charmed circle in the summer twilight. As sunset over Brownsea Island wanes, those little beady lights all round the rim of the harbour twinkle into life. And night follows.

The lighted paddle steamers, free of their crowded excursionists, come in through the dusk and pass up to their moorings at Poole. On windy nights their wash is hardly noticed; in a calm they set things rolling as if the roll will never end. Loitering on deck when the night is clear, one can watch the wheeling beam in the sky from St. Catherine's light, five and twenty miles distant. The light itself is below the horizon, and the horizon is behind the sandhills.

．　　．　　．　　．　　．　　．

From Sandbanks the lure of the sea always coaxes me outside. I doubt whether I have ever up-anchored from Sandbanks and sailed to Poole. My arrivals at Poole have always been straight from the sea.

One evening, for instance, the yacht had been sailing westward in the Solent between a sunset and a rising moon. At midnight she was off Hengistbury Head, ghosting along in a sort of wonder-world of moonlit water; at one (a.m.) she

BALLARD DOWN, SWANAGE

was becalmed off Boscombe Cliffs. Mist was now
gathering and the moonlight flooded through it ;
the sea meanwhile had become almost oily calm.
Down went the anchor ; and the ship's company,
after lounging on deck until well after two (unable
to forgo the charm of it all), dropped below and
slept.

A brisk southerly breeze brought me on deck at
about nine. Those earthy cliffs at Boscombe, just
beside us, were bright in sunshine, and *Growler*
was rocking merrily. Poole was ours for the taking
at any moment with this commanding breeze ; we
could enter against the strength of the ebb if we
chose. But there was no object in coming to
anchor early in the day, and away we went beating
over a lumpy seaway from Bournemouth to Swanage.
The spray flew. Bournemouth and the pine-clad
Canford Cliffs receded and were gone. The tide-
rip off old Harry was strong, with breaking seas ;
off Ballard Down—although the wind was full on
shore—the sea was much quieter.

Then, wet and salty-faced, we put the helm up
and raced back from Swanage into the tide-rip
again, which gave us a regular dusting, the yacht
sheering extravagantly and the dinghy gone mad.
In a lather of soap-suds we were blown, heaving
and heaving, up to the harbour entrance, and we
drove rollicking through. Then, of a sudden, a
calm had fallen on the water, and the yacht sailed
with even speed. She was in.

With so steady a breeze, she was soon up the main
channel to Poole.

POOLE QUAY

Obviously, in a natural harbour as good as this, a seaport in earlier centuries was inevitable. The creek at the mouth of Holes Bay, licking, as it does, round the hard shore itself, with no mud-flats between, suggested the proper site. And here is Poole.

Alfred built ships here, Canute used it as a port; under the Normans it had its first charter; it sent ships for Edward III's siege of Calais, and so on. Leland says that Richard III " began a pece of a town waulle at one end of the Kay, and promised large things to the town of Pole." " Pole " fitted out several ships to fight the Armada, and the town's prosperity was continuous into the nineteenth century.

The port was noted a century ago for its Newfoundland trade. Newfoundland, our oldest Colony, is said to have been first colonised by Poole men. The harbour was, in those days, full of square-riggers, and they must have been wonderfully handled in the narrow tideway. Nowadays, the larger sailing ships (small beside the Newfoundlanders) generally take a tug. I have seen more than one of them which has attempted to turn to windward under sail fail to manage it. She has taken the putty, and stayed there for a tide or two.

Defoe mentioned Poole as being famous for oysters, and added that " more pearls are found in the Poole oysters, and larger, than in any other oysters about England."

The wind had now settled in the south-east and was breezing up. The anchorage off Poole was

STUDLAND FROM POOLE CHANNEL

therefore at a discount. It would, of course, be possible to go through the swing-bridge into Holes Bay, and bring up there in shelter. That, however, I have only done when proposing to leave the yacht at Poole for a time ; the trouble of negotiating the swing-bridge is not otherwise worth while. I have also sailed up Holes Bay, but it really leads nowhere. So this evening we sailed in the dusk up to Russell Quay, away in the wilds, beside the heathered slopes of Arne.

The one place beyond was Wareham, and Wareham is delightful. The deep-water channel, leading to it through the shallows of the upper harbour, is narrow, but it is well enough marked. It leads to the River Frome, and the voyage is finished by way of a winding inland river, reed-bordered. This change, after the sea, has its own charm. The yacht can moor beside the bank, Broads fashion ; and the water is fresh water, fit to wash in. This is the only place in Solent waters (so far as I know) where —in waters continuous with the salt sea—the full transition to the fresh water is achieved.

The red cliff at Wareham is a curious feature ; tree-clad on top, its face towards the river is bare and abrupt as a sea-cliff.

Wareham itself is ancient beyond the ordinary. It is still a walled town, its walls being—not masonry —but embankments of earth. These walls were here long before the Romans came, and they are still here. They were thrown up (it is thought) by the ancient Britons, or by some peoples earlier still. The walls themselves are now rounded and

LORD HOWE'S SHIPS OF THE
GLORIOUS FIRST OF JUNE

JUST BEFORE SUNRISE

grass-grown, enclosing a rectangular town, with streets arranged on a rectangular plan, and the town lies foursquare between the rivers Frome and Trent (or Piddle), which are parallel at this spot :

> The *Piddle* that this while bestir'd her nimble feet,
> In falling to the *Poole* her sister *Froome* to meet.

Beside the river bank *Growler* has lain moored, the lush meadows beside her, and the Purbeck Hills, with Creech Barrow, grouped on the skyline. The ancient town is close at hand.

From a quiet berth here I watched the sunset behind Wareham. Plovers circled, with their plaintive cry, in the twilight, and the image of the yacht was perfect in the river. A light mist was over the flat land. Then I took a turn ashore along the bank and loitered towards Red Cliff ; and suddenly, on passing the hill, I came face to face with the red moon which had risen. Thickets on the hill-side were silhouetted against the gold face. I stood there alone ; the night was completely without sound.

# CHAPTER XIII

## ROUND ST. CATHERINE'S

WE had brought up in Studland Bay overnight because the south-westerly wind was so boisterous. Inside Poole Harbour, off Sandbanks or Hamworthy, we could have lain, had we chosen, but we should have been less comfortable. In Studland it sometimes seems that, the stronger the wind, the snugger the berth. The wind had been knocking up a vicious seaway outside, but it left Studland calm; it streaked viciously over the surface of the water here, but that was all. The fact is curious. A wind offshore, when really strong, seems to keep the swell out of the bay. The moment the wind moderates, in comes the swell; and the yacht, which had lain rock-steady during the heavy blow, begins to toss and roll in the calm.

In a grey morning to-day the yacht was rocking lightly, for the heavy blow had abated, and the Isle of Wight was now invisible in distant haze. We made sharp work of our breakfast, and shortened the cable. The anchor was soon on board, and we were away for the invisible Island, laying a course east by south. The downs began to pile higher and higher astern of us over the low Studland Cliffs, dwarfing them; and we were well away into the open, with a sterling breeze.

The swell that was running from yesterday's

storm-wind was quite imposing still, and we were rollicking along with a roll and a toss over it. This was good and jovial progress. But it was only good while it lasted, and the fact is that it failed to last long. The wind lost its confidence, and, after a few expiring puffs, dropped into a mere ghost of an air.

"Well, hang it," I protested, "I did *not* expect this. The glass wasn't rising; it's even falling a little, and—here, *look* at the sails!"

Look at them, indeed! They merely flapped and cracked. The wind had gone, but the swell had not. We lay becalmed; and the boom thumped and banged heavily to and fro as we rolled.

"One of the few *really* unattractive things in sailing. Beastly!" I said it with conviction, as I steadied myself against the deep roll, and kept my head ducked to clear that flogging boom.

A gleam of sunshine lit up the low coastline some five miles away to northward; and the square tower of Christchurch Priory (a very tiny square, tucked in there behind Hengistbury Head) sprang into light for a moment against a skyline of dark distance. It was all a long way off.

Christchurch Harbour was probably less inaccessible in the past than now. Camden, exploring "Hantshire" in the reign of Elizabeth, found the town a seaport. "At conflux of two rivers is a small populous seaport, now, from its church dedicated to Christ, called *Christ Church*, antiently from its situation between two rivers *Twinamburne*, in the same sense as *Interamna* in Italy. It was

once defended by a castle and adorned with an
antient church and prebendaries, built in Saxon
times."

The gleam passed and left Christchurch grey, and
the seaway rather sullen. The boom flogged and
banged. And the yacht rolled.

" Silly business ! We should have saved our tide
round St. Catherine's if this hadn't happened, and
now—well, we're here, and going to stay here."

I tapped the glass, and it sluggishly fell a little
more.

" The calm won't last," I predicted. " We
may have all the wind we want and more before
the day's out."

Almost as I spoke a light air stirred from the
west, nearly due astern. It seemed holding.

" Come on, let's make the most of it," I said ;
and, nothing loth to have a job to do, we ran out the
long boathook as a spinnaker boom, and set the big
jib and staysail as spinnaker. The yacht wallowed
all the time, putting first the boom in the water
on one side and then rolling over to put the
spinnaker boom in on the other. Foothold was
precarious, in spite of the calm.

Lost labour ! Here came the true breeze,
crisping and whitening the wave-crests—a sou'-
wester. In we brought the makeshift spinnaker
in a hurry, and the yacht was got into proper trim
again in quick time. This was a living breeze
now, and the island, invisible no longer, was clean-
cut and jewel-like in a new shaft of sunlight.
*Growler* gathered speed and the miles began to

CHRISTCHURCH

fly.   She still rolled, but the roll was more equable ;
the sense of wallowing, and the jerk of the boom
as it *wrenched* at its sheet, had gone.   This was
splendid.

The outlook had changed at a stroke.   For the
time being there was sunshine ;  but quite a strong
wind was blowing round our ears.   The waves
topped in a genial and unthreatening way, with just
a crest of white foam and no more.   Sometimes a
" fair-weather flop " might catch us on the quarter,
throwing a little water on board, but nothing
beyond that.   We were raising the Island all the
time, as splendid a landfall as one could wish, its
steep white cliffs in sun and shadow.

Our   true   course   would   have   been   for   St.
Catherine's, but we stood straight to the Needles,
for the sake of the splendid view.   We took our
chance of the wind falling ;  the tidal indraught
into Freshwater Bay might be a nuisance if it did,
but the wind seemed sure enough.

Nearer, nearer came the superb cliff-face.   We
were in the fairway for the Needles Channel and
the Solent.   Then the tiller was shoved down the
least trifle, and we had left the fairway and had
turned southward to the Bridge (the under-water
reef beyond the Needles).   The Needles Rocks soon
stretched themselves—white in sunshine—between
us and the Solent.   Dead white against clouds
which were lowering and gloomy, they went by us,
and were soon on our quarter ;  the great cliff of
Scratchells had heaped up on our beam, close
aboard, and the waves were breaking at the foot.

THE NEEDLES

The long cliff-face of chalk, crannied and flint-barred, stretched onward toward Freshwater.

The breeze was stiff and the sea was alive. Powerfully the yacht swung over the long, steep ridges. Headed now for St. Catherine's Point, she was crossing the Bay.

The indraught is of no account save in thick weather and calms. Grenville Collins, in the reign of Charles II, wrote of it thus: " There is a strong Indraught that sets in at the *Needles* and into *Pool*; which Indraught hath hauld many Ships into

*Fresh-water Bay*. But I think it, and I am sure, that no Ship can run ashoar in *Fresh-water Bay*, if they did but mind the Lead; the neglect of which hath been the loss of many Ships. Keep a five and twenty and thirty Fathom water, and you need not fear the Indraught of the *Wight*."

That instruction, of course, is for deep-water vessels or coasters making a passage. It would keep them twenty miles offshore, a counsel of safety in thick weather, for the indraught is very definite when winds are light. A small example of it can constantly be observed. On the down above the Needles is a golf-course, and the balls, sometimes caught by the wind or badly driven, fly over the cliff-edge, and fall sheer into the sea. The tide does not sweep them away to St. Catherine's; it washes them up on the beach between Brook and Afton. The small Island-boys know it well; and the balls are not altogether wasted.

Old shipmasters, working by rule of thumb, were often very hazy about their landfalls, especially after storms which had caused them to heave to for some days. Even ships which had successfully " struck soundings in the Channel of old England " after crossing the Atlantic, made serious mistakes in the Channel itself. In 1785, Samuel Kelly recorded what happened when he was an apprentice on a ship homeward bound which had " gained the English Channel and passed Plymouth " :

" One morning as I came on deck I found our ship hauling in round St. Alban's head, our master supposing it to be the Isle of Wight. I looked

again and again at the place, but the view was
quite unknown to me, and I declared it was not
the place he supposed it to be, and on looking to the
eastward he perceived the Wight, and as the wind

PAST FRESHWATER DOWN
(SCRATCHELLS BAY ON LEFT)

was fair we entered the Needles about nine in the
morning, and anchored to my great joy at Spithead
about noon, some day the latter end of September,
1785."

It was rather a casual way of coming home ; but

exactly the same thing used to happen at Beachy Head. Shipmasters were wont to mistake the headland for the South Foreland, and they altered course and carried on—as they believed—for the Thames, until they were picked up by the Royal Sovereign or some other shoal in Pevensey Bay. The very name of the Royal Sovereign shoal is borrowed from a first-rate of that name wrecked there in the days of sail.

Methods with the coasting shipmasters were primitive enough ; they knew their own usual tracks, but once blown off them were completely lost. Samuel Kelly recalls an instance when he was in a coaster in the Bristol Channel : " During the passage, the captain was applied to for a chart that we might compute our distance from the headland, to which he replied there had never been such a thing on board the vessel, which I believe was full thirty years old."

Making towards St. Catherine's, as we were to-day (though perhaps on a different bearing), home-ward bounders of that era would be shaping course for Spithead, and would soon be round the corner and shortening sail. In heavy weather the work aloft in oilskins and sea-boots was no comfortable task, but there would be no green hands on the deep-water vessel making her landfall here ; the youngsters who swung themselves up the futtock-shrouds, from the lower rigging into the top, would think with scorn of their own selves of yesteryear. Outward bound—they had perhaps to be driven up the rigging with an old sailor behind them to catch them if they lost their nerve at that awkward moment of swinging, half upside-down, from the futtock-shrouds into the top.

It was severe work for the novice, even when kindly trained. And the cruelty of it in a " hell-ship," when a bucko mate was knocking about a crew of shanghaied " hoboes " with a belaying-pin, or driving them aloft with a knuckle-duster, must have surpassed description. Among the Western Ocean packets, the Black Ball liners had perhaps the worst reputation. The old crew would have jumped the vessel the moment she touched land. Then the crimps put a full new crew on board ; and, where seamen were lacking, a few doped landsmen were thrown in, and sometimes even a corpse was put on board (" Drunk now, but will be all right in the morning, Captain "), to make up the number.

> With the tinkers and tailors and soldiers and all
>    (*To my yeo, ho !   Blow the man down !*)
> That ship for prime seamen on board a Black Ball,
>    (*Oh, give me some time to blow the man down !*)

So said the shanty ; and " When a Black Baller is clear of the land," then :

> " Lay aft," is the cry, " to the break of the poop ! "
>    (*To my yeo, ho !   Blow the man down !*)
> " Or I'll help you along with the toe of my boot,"

and so on ; and then :

> ' Tis larboard and starboard on the deck you will sprawl,
> For " Kicking Jack Williams " commands that Black Ball
>    (*Oh, give me some time to blow the man down !*)

Fancy the nineteenth-century experiences of a pampered landsman. Doped among friends at some friendly bar ashore, he would sleep happily, only to be awakened with the heavy toe of a sea-boot and a bucket of water, to stagger up and be knocked flat again with a horny fist! It was not so long ago, either.

The yacht was romping on. Freshwater, deep in the curve of the Bay, had long gone by, and the chalk faces were past. The low earth cliffs of Brook and Atherfield were abeam now; seen from the beach they look high enough, but they are dwarfed and insignificant when, from the sea, the great downs are behind and above them.

All the glitter had faded from the day. The brief sunlight was lost. Heavy clouds had completely mastered it, and the seaway was dirty grey. The seas were inclined to break, and a little green water bumped on board now and again. But the yacht's speed was swift and assured now; she would easily save her tide round the Point.

"Good going—this! Watch the buoy off Atherfield Ledges running along the shore."

The buoy was being passed in grand style, and alignment of objects on shore showed also a very healthy turn of speed.

Chale and Blackgang were there, dark and forbidding; the whole bay is a cruel lee-shore when

> leaps ashore the full sou' west
> All heavy-winged with brine.

"Keep her offshore!" I called to my shipmate, now at the helm; "give the Point a berth."

He was gripping the tiller, which kicked heavily

ST. CATHERINE'S TO VENTNOR
(WITH CULVER CLIFF JUST OPENING)

now and again.  He shoved it over with both hands, turning her more offshore.

The race off St. Catherine's is rather an unaccountable affair, being sometimes tame and sometimes very mutinous.  It is of much less account than that of St. Albans, but of longer duration; it lasts all the way from St. Catherine's to Dunnose, near Shanklin.  The race was in friendly mood today, though it would become more troublesome when the tide turned.  And it *can* be quite nasty when it likes.

We had hauled the Point abeam and the coast was changing every instant; Bonchurch Down was there, sloping toward the abrupt fall of Dunnose. A new reach of coast had taken the place of St. Catherine's, and there, beyond Dunnose, was the gracious white line of Culver, on the horizon.

"This race is a paltry affair to-day," I said; "let's stand inshore and look at the country; there's lots of water."

So, with heed, for the wind was now almost dead aft, and we ran the risk of a gybe, we shaped course closer inshore, scanning the broken dark cliffs with their ragged belt of wood below that velvet smoothness of the down. The landfall was stern, but it was noble.

*Growler* rose and fell over the small, breaking hills of sea, and swept rapidly on. There was Ventnor, nestling below the down, and Dunnose, over the bows, was abrupt and solid.

"Pity there isn't a glimpse of sunlight now; the picture wants it."

As if at the word, sunlight came a moment later —a flood of life over everything. We had just hauled Dunnose abeam when that fairy wand touched the seascape. In a trice, the dingy sea had glittered into living blue, and the clouds above had soon rolled up and gone.

The wind was stronger with the clearing, and had shifted a little, coming, in a most tiresome fashion, dead aft again. We rigged a boom-tackle, to prevent an accidental gybe in these following seas, for they tossed the yacht like a cork, making her sheer quite a great deal, despite the helmsman's best efforts. The dinghy, of course, was a nuisance, first trying to come on board on the white crest of a great wave, and then dropping back with a *crack* that threatened to part both her painters.

Across Sandown Bay, we shaped course for Culver;

and Shanklin and Sandown lay in the hollow of the curve. The dark sea was flecked with a scatter of foam-caps everywhere; and we were raising the white wall of sunlit Culver every moment, over the rolling blue.

"Confounded nuisance, the dinghy," my ship-mate commented. "Sure to be some fly in the ointment," he added; "but it's a perfect paradise, this—in the matter of sailing, apart from the little brute."

The waves topped more and more off the Point. The white cliff was now beside us. The dinghy did her puny best to give trouble, but the wind drove us gallantly on, on, on, and the dinghy still followed.

Course was shaped for Bembridge Ledge, which I intended crossing. I had calculated the state of tide, and was satisfied that I could cut the corner.

The local name of the reef of rocks used to be Dicky Daw's Rocks, and Dicky Daw's name has even found its way into the charts.

Dicky Daw was a local smuggler, living at Bembridge. Once, when pursued by revenue cutters, sailing close-hauled, he laid his own course through a deeper gut inside the ledge. The revenue cutters were obliged to go about, in order to weather the ledge; and so Dicky Daw escaped.

We were sailing straight over the ledge itself to-day. It is all very well, with a light-draught vessel that will float on a heavy dew (so to speak) to cut corners over mud-banks, with only a narrow margin to spare; there is no anxiety. Rocks are a different matter. We were quite all right, but I was glad to be over. The yacht draws one foot ten inches with lee-boards raised, and I expected to find four feet six inches at least on the ledge. The pace was headlong, and the water (almost smooth in shelter here) clear as crystal, so that the rocks looked closer than they were as they jumped up suddenly out of the deeper greeny-blue when we reached the edge of the reef. Nearer, nearer, nearer the surface they came as we raced over them. Had I miscalculated? They would well-nigh tear the bottom out of her, passing at this pace. I jabbed down the boathook now and again; and its iron-head rang metallically on the rocks; but the depth was sufficient—just, in fact, as I had figured it. I felt little real doubt, but the very thought set one's teeth on edge. We were over, and I breathed perhaps more freely.

"See the *Majestic*!" Out from Spithead came the great liner, outward bound for New York; and afternoon sunlight was becoming more golden toward evening as we romped past the Nomans Fort and across to the Spit Sand Fort and the fairway for Portsmouth.

"The tide's against us," I said. "It doesn't matter here. But when Gosport cuts off the breeze at the bottle-neck just where the tide is strongest—well, I wonder."

We had discussed it before, and had decided that we would make a shot at Portsmouth; and, if we failed, drop back across to Seaview and anchor there.

We drove solidly and confidently into the entrance, and then a sudden brake seemed to be put on, smooth as butter, but sure as fate. We had stopped. The Gosport buildings had taken our wind ; we not only stopped, but slid smoothly sternwards a little. Then we slid a little more, until we opened out sufficiently to get the breeze again, which put us back into the bottle-neck. Little groups of people on shore stood to watch us, as—with the blue water sluicing past her, and a strong wave of foam breaking under her forefoot— *Growler* hung, poised, unable to stir, right in the fairway.

Then, creeping in over the Spit Sand to cheat the tide, came a local barge, and tried to shoot the entrance.

" Now we'll see," I said, " what a bit more local knowledge can do."

Seemingly, it could not do much ; for the barge shot as far as we had shot, and no more. Two of us now hung, suspended, as if some enchanter had put a spell upon us both. The tide-water still sluiced out, seaward.

Patience and perseverance won the day ; and at last, with a quicker little spurt of speed, at the two-hundredth attempt, *Growler* won through the bottle-neck into the breeze beyond, and she was soon smoothly mastering the tide up the Harbour. That barge—as it happened—was still captive, and did not make her escape until a quarter of an hour later. We kept looking back at her as we skimmed up the harbour.

In the late summer dusk we anchored off Porchester at nine p.m., exactly twelve hours after we had got our anchor off Studland.

# CHAPTER XIV

## PORTSMOUTH HARBOUR

IT often happens that one's first visit to a place remains more strongly marked in memory than any other. Porchester, with me, is a case in point ; and I must go back a few years to recall the occasion.

THE ENTRANCE AT PORTSMOUTH

On a summer evening we had been bound for Portsmouth Harbour from the Western Solent. The wind was fair, and we had had a lazy time, while, running free with an easy swing in her movement, the yacht had spilled the miles smoothly astern. It had been good.

194

But we needed now to bestir ourselves a little, for the entrance to Portsmouth is narrow and busy. Past Southsea Castle, we were soon inside. Though the harbour is crowded with shipping—vessels anchored and moored and berthed, packet ships, ships of war, yachts, tugs, ferries—yet the fairway is kept punctiliously clear. It teems only with its own unceasing traffic. With wind and tide, we romped past the Harbour Station and the Royal Yacht. The waters on every hand were thick with mooring buoys and grey vessels of war.

Bound as we were for Porchester, we were going up to the real source of things—to the original port; for Portsmouth was once only the gateway and approach for the great Portus Adurni. Portcestre, or Porchester as it is now written, was the parent place.

Porchester Lake of the present day is well marked, with black and chequer posts. Cloud-shadows streaked the landscape, and—as we approached it —Porchester Castle stood blue in shadow. Portsdown Hill, the chalk down behind, was in sunlight.

We brought up right beside the castle wall and furled our sails; here we would remain. The work of snugging down and the routine of the evening meal occupied the last hour of daylight, so that the sun had set and dusk was upon us before we were ready to pull ashore in the dinghy. We landed at the little hard which was close aboard of us.

"It's marvellously alone—the old castle," my shipmate said, as we set foot ashore in the twilight.

Not a living soul was in sight, and there it was—
the Norman keep above the Roman east wall and
watergate. All was deserted and silent. It had
been an impressive approach ; the castle seemed to
daunt one somehow with its aloofness and indiffer-
ence.

" Portsmouth I know well enough, but I've never
penetrated here before. I fancied, I suppose, the
smoke would be up here too and the fairway cluttered up with dockyard cast-offs. I was wrong."
Once ashore, we had drawn right away from modern
influences ; and, as we tied up the dinghy and
looked about us in that summer dusk, we had a
sense akin to wonder. We passed landward by a
grassy path, and the place—deserted utterly—was
still our own.

Porchester was one of the Roman strongholds of
the Saxon Shore, and was then situated in a great
forest—the Forest of Bere. But its history is
obscure for many centuries. The Normans adopted
it, and built the keep, and the castle was often
visited by Plantagenet kings, John in particular.
Edward I, Edward III, and Henry V all embarked
from its watergate for campaigns in France ; Richard
II built its King's Hall and Great Hall, and so the
story went on. It is now derelict entirely—a ruin.
Grass and ivy are everywhere.

We wandered around it again next morning, but
did not better our first idea of it ; its grandeur had
overshadowed us in that sombre dusk, and the
enchantment of the earlier impression is the impression that remains.

PORCHESTER CASTLE AND PORTSDOWN HILL.

We waited until afternoon to make sail for Fareham, dropping down Porchester Lake on the tail of the ebb in order to carry the young flood with us up Fareham way. While the tide was as low as this, our space for beating among the moored vessels at the mouth of the Lake was not liberal, but we found more room down by Priddy's Hard and the Ferry. We were only loitering. The young

flood had not yet begun to make, and in the meantime we would stand off and on among these steel
hulls at moorings.

" Ugly brutes ! Look at that chap—the bulges
may be useful, but they ain't pretty ; then the
hull's eaten up with rust, and the steel top-hamper's
half dismantled. What a picture ! "

The long silhouette of Portsmouth, viewed from
Porchester Lake, is one of chimneys and factory
roofs and great lattice cranes. You can hardly
conjure the vision of the old Portsmouth of sail-
lofts and rope-walks. The waterside certainly has
its relics of the past ; but, even so, a harbour
crowded with sail is now difficult to picture. There
are old prints in plenty that show it ; a fine sight
it must have been.

Seen from Spithead, however, with that old
tower at its entrance and the masts beyond,
the place is much less different from the old
idea.

Portsmouth is (as already noted) of more recent
origin than Southampton ; and—though a small
town had existed since the Conquest—Portsmouth
achieved no real importance until the reign of
Henry VIII.

It had, nevertheless, been a place of landing and
embarkation in its early years ; and in 1101 Robert
of Normandy landed here, hoping to make good
his claim to the throne of England. As a naval
port it was tributary—through the Middle Ages—
to Southampton. The royal galleys were based on
Portsmouth in 1213, and royal ships were laid up

in its creeks. These were the beginnings. Portsmouth was, however, more open to attack than the parent port, and was frequently plundered and burnt by the French. Indeed, for the eight years following 1341 it was exempted from taxation owing to the damage suffered. Its openness to attack probably delayed its development until after it had been regularly fortified in 1415.

Looking soberly back at the beginnings of Portsmouth one has to admit that any modern ugliness must not be resented. For this ugliness appertains to what has really always been its essential quality. Pioneer development of the shore-side appliances of shipping created Portsmouth. When ships were smaller, they were built in a meadow, launched, and done with. Now they require factories to make their parts and docks to hold them.

The process began in 1212, when the Sheriff of Southampton received an order to cause the docks of Portsmouth " to be inclosed with a strong wall for the preservation of the King's Ships and Galleys," and to erect pent-houses for the tackle of the galleys. " Docks " were not then so elaborate as their modern counterparts. When a ship was to be laid up, she was towed up some handy natural creek at the top of the tide ; and, as the tide went down, men set to work to build a wall across the berth selected, and thus keep out the tide at its next high water. The ship was thus left in a dry dock ; and docks of that character sufficed for 250 years.

In 1495, when Henry VII was King, the dock,

though remaining the same in principle, was developed. Brigandine was the man sent down by the King to Portsmouth, and he built a new dry dock. It had double gates, and the space between was filled with clay. In 1496 twenty men were at work " at every tide both day and night, weying up of the piles and shorys and digging of ye clay and other rubbish between ye gates." In 1523 the dock was increased in size, to enable the *Henry Grâce à Dieu* to be brought in.

Coming thus to the time of Henry VIII, one must, of course, look to see what Leland says. Leland was evidently impressed with the defences of the harbour entrance. " There is at this point of the haven," he says, " a great round tower, almost double in quantity and strength to that which is on the west side of the haven, right opposite to it, and here is a mighty chain of iron to draw from tower to tower."

He adds that " the town is muried " (walled) " with a mud wall, armed with timber whereon are great pieces of iron and brass ordnance." The wall also had " a ditch without it."

During his first wars with France, Henry VIII erected three great brewing houses, with implements to serve his ships at such times as they should go to sea in time of war. The town of Portsmouth was " bare and little occupied in time of peace."

The port lost, under Elizabeth, its new-found eminence, for Deptford became the favoured place, and ships in commission were sent to lie in the Medway and Thames. In the reign of Charles I

IN PORTSMOUTH · HARBOUR

Buckingham's fleet lay here when Buckingham was stabbed by Felton, but not until the Civil War (when Portsmouth declared for the Parliament) did the dockyard town again become really important.

This declaration for Parliament was not surprising, for a radical spirit had shown itself in Portsmouth on many occasions. As far back as 1539 a case of insubordination in the fleet occurred, when a sailor—examined for mutinous language—was charged with saying that if his blood and the King's were both in a dish there would be no difference between them; and also that " if the Great Turk would give him a penny a day more he would serve him "—sentiments which (as Mr. Carr Laughton, recounting the incident, dryly observes) " were both rather out of place in Portsmouth of that date."

There were mutinies also (generally through systematic neglect of the fleet in the matter of food and pay), and there was penal discipline to match. But the first instance recorded of " flogging round the fleet " had no reference to insubordination. A carpenter's mate on H.M.S. *Swiftsure*, in 1653, charged with drunkenness, swearing, and uncleanness, was sentenced to receive ten lashes with a whip by the side of each flagship present, and there was to be written a paper on his hat stating his crime, and the drum beating in the boat's head. He was then towed at the boat's stern to Gosport.

The full punishment of flogging through the Fleet involved a certain number of lashes beside every ship assembled. Few men—it is said—were strong enough to survive ; and if they survived they were wrecks for life. Sometimes the alternative of the gallows was offered.

But ordinary flogging was quite a usual occurrence. The victim, stripped to the waist, was tied to a grating ; the executioner was a powerful seaman, and the weapon the cat—with its heavy tails of knotted cord. The first blow flayed the skin from the man's back, and six or a dozen made it a slough of blood. Three dozen was the common punishment, and three hundred were often given.

Cases of the capital penalty were frequent enough. The execution of James Aitken in 1776, for trying to set fire to the dockyard, had the traditional setting : it recalls Treasure Island. "You've seen 'em, maybe, hanged in chains, birds about 'em, seamen p'inting 'em out as they go down with the tide. . . . And you can hear the chains a-jangle as you go about and reach for the other buoy." James Aitken was hanged on a gallows sixty feet high, and then suspended˙ in chains at the Blockhouse Fort, that all going in and out of the harbour might bear his fate in mind. His bones hung there bleaching for a long time, until finally some sailors cut down the skeleton and used it to pay an alehouse score.

An instance (happily a solitary one) of misplaced discipline in the very highest quarters occurred at Portsmouth in 1757: the famous case of Admiral Byng. Byng was tried on board the *Monarque*, unjustly accused of not having done his utmost to prevent the loss of Minorca to England, and he was found guilty. He appeared on the quarter-deck, bandaged his own eyes, and gave the signal to the Marines by the dropping of a handkerchief. Only three minutes elapsed from time the admiral came on deck until he fell, pierced by five bullets. " Dans ce pays-ci," said Voltaire, " il est bon de tuer de temps en temps un amiral, pour encourager les autres."

But it is not history of trials and executions that one wants to recall ; rather it is the vision of white-sailed vessels that used this fairway, out and in. In 1588 the *Rat of Wight*, eighty tons, sailed in with the news of the sailing of the Armada from Lisbon, and of its putting back into Corunna. In the same year the Queen's ships *Hope*, *Nonpareil*, and *Advice* were fitted out, and sailed with Drake to Plymouth. In 1652 Blake brought in his crippled ships and wounded men after a battle off the Isle of Wight ; he came ashore himself with a splinter in his thigh, and made a slow recovery, his health being poor. Then, in 1744, Anson returned in the *Centurion* from his amazing voyage and landed his treasure for conveyance to London ; Hawke brought his prizes from Quiberon Bay, and Howe from the Glorious First of June. In 1803 Nelson hoisted his flag on board the *Victory*, proceeding to the blockade of Toulon. On the 15th of September, 1805, he sailed again.

It was Nelson's last farewell to England. " He reached Portsmouth " (wrote Southey), " and, having despatched his business on shore, endeavoured to elude the populace by taking a by-way to the beach ; but a crowd collected in his train, pressing forward to obtain sight of his face ; many

TWILIGHT AT FAREHAM

were in tears, and many knelt down before him and blessed him as he passed. England has had many heroes, but never one who so entirely possessed the love of his fellow-countrymen as Nelson. . . . They pressed upon the parapet to gaze after him when his barge pushed off, and he was returning their cheers by waving his hat."

"I had their huzzas before," said Nelson to Hardy, who sat beside him in the boat; "now I have their hearts."

When the *Victory* returned, Nelson's work had

been completed. " The outstanding and pre-
dominant feature " of Trafalgar—it has been justly
said—was " its finality." Nothing remained to be
done ; and the dead admiral lay, embalmed for
burial, on board his flagship when she came home.

With the young flood, we were bound this evening
for Fareham. This channel—in which men-of-war
still lie—has accommodated many ships in its time.
But enough of history. Suffice it merely to recall
the figure of Shipbuilder Pett, who was sent to
Portsmouth in King Charles II's reign to report upon
the harbour. Some question had arisen as to
whether " worm destructive to ships " were bred in
Portsmouth Harbour ; Pett believed not, but
recommended that men-of-war should lie in Fareham Channel. And in Fareham Channel accordingly the King's ships lay.

In the evening sunlight we sailed on ; the wind
was falling lighter, and, after we had left astern
those grey modern hulls at moorings, our progress
was slow. Past Bedenham Pier the channel grew
narrower, for the tide had not yet broadened over
the flats ; and beyond the last bend at Fleetland
there was no room at all. With the best will in
the world to keep going, we stopped—for we went
aground.

We tied up to a post to await better water ; and
while we lay the light wind dwindled with the sun-
down, and was gone. With the sweep worked
lazily as soon as we floated, just to give us bare
steering-way, we drifted in the twilight up to
Fareham.

# CHAPTER XV

## CHICHESTER AND LANGSTON

IT was from Portsmouth Harbour that we moved on to Chichester, but not from Fareham. Many things—trivial, pleasant, and unrecorded—had occurred between. And Portsmouth Harbour itself was (as it happened) an unexpected starting-place.

The yacht had been away somewhere down the Western Solent. By the light of the setting moon that morning, we got under way before sunrise, Lymington way. The idea had been to sail to Bembridge, put in there for the night, and shift across to Chichester the following forenoon.

"The act of turning out of a warm bunk at three in the morning is hateful," I said to a shipmate who was equally sleepy-eyed, as we stood and yawned in the well; "but once the deed is done it's always well worth while."

It is; and never more so than it was this morning. The full moon was low in the sky, and the breeze was light but steady. We were soon away.

"It makes good going, even to windward, when you have a racing tide under you and a breeze like this." The breeze was enough to keep the yacht thoroughly alive, yet it was not hard enough to knock up breaking waves to stop her. Conditions were perfect.

I put the helm down and she came about. The

breeze was easterly, and we should have to beat all
the way ; but that is all in the game, and the game
was seen at its pleasantest this morning. First
flush of dawn was warming the eastern sky, and
that great moon astern was really setting now. In
the dawn twilight the helmsman was sailing heedfully in order to get the last ounce of progress
possible. There might be a race with time to
catch the tide for Bembridge ; and that, too, was
all in the game.

The sun came up, a red ball, when the yacht was
off Needs Oar. Unfortunately, with sunrise the
best of the day was over, for grey cloud worked
across the sky and toned everything to a low key of
grey. The wind, too, was less dependable. By
the time that we had struggled along to Ryde it
had become clear that we could not save our tide
to Bembridge. The wind was breezing up hard
now from the south-east, but this stronger wind
was too late for us ; there was no chance of making
Bembridge until late this evening.

"We've got to pull a reef down now."

The wind was blowing up strongly past Nettlestone
Point. By working to and fro over the Ryde Sand
we were able to cheat the tide a little and to keep
out of the rougher water ; but the falling tide
would soon drive us off into the main channel, and
there was not one chance of weathering the Nomans
Fort.

"What now ? "

The yacht was lively—very lively.

She was well able to sail violently to and fro, but

OLD HARRY ROCKS

PASSING DUNNOSE

for several hours to come she could do no more than maintain the distance already won—if she could manage that. The tide was sucking her back, by the beam. True, she could anchor, but a berth here would be one of amazing discomfort. Drop back for shelter ? No, that went against the grain too much.

In the circumstances, Portsmouth offered the best solution. But even Portsmouth was not a perfectly easy entrance to-day for a yacht towing a dinghy. The ebb was racing out of the narrow entrance, and the hard wind—blowing against it— was scooping the steep-breaking waves that one knows so well. The dinghy was already on two painters and this brief passage would test painters to the utmost.

" Stay her round ; don't gybe her in this wind."

Round she came. Instead of the thud, thud, thud of the breaking waves on a yacht close-hauled, there was now the lift and drop of the following seas. The yacht was headed for Portsmouth, and she was sheering extravagantly, having—with her light draught—little hold on the water.

" Kicks ? Watch her ! " I said it through clenched teeth, as the tiller—though grasped in both hands—gave me body-blows fit to bruise my ribs. The yacht was racing headlong for the harbour. Knocked up in a few hours, this welter of foam was everywhere. Entrance, as one knew by experience already, is as a rule difficult against a tide ; but not to-day. The wind was completely master, and the yacht went staggering and toppling in. I was glad to be inside with the dinghy still there, intact. We brought up in Porchester Lake, clear of the traffic, and in decent shelter.

.    .    .    .    .

Next morning, also, an early start would be necessary ; but I had in mind that I would not start at all for Chichester if the wind were as strong as this from the south-east. The seas were dangerous enough for a dinghy in tow even in the deep entrance to Portsmouth ; in the shoal entrance to Chichester they would be much worse. Even apart from the dinghy, moreover, the seas there might easily threaten the yacht herself. Neither Langston nor Chichester should be approached when a heavy sea is running. " In rough weather " (the *Channel Pilot* says), " if there is any swell outside, there is one sheet of broken water with heavy rollers." The approaches of Langston and Chichester are dangerous places then.

I was full of doubts at three in the morning. Through the darkness the wind came, full-bodied ; the dark water was creased and furrowed with it. Wind, moreover, so often gathers weight after daybreak.

"What about it ? It means a dirty little passage, and then perhaps we shall funk the entrance when we get there."

The thing was worth a trial anyway, and we got the tiers off the mainsail. I had been in and out of Chichester often before, and the fact of knowing the way was a definite advantage. The anchor clanked against the bobstay, and was brought on board. Between the tall posts that mark the channel, the yacht made her way seaward.

" Either the buildings of Portsmouth are keeping the wind off us, or the wind has fallen very much lighter."

The long silhouette of Portsmouth, with its tall chimneys and lattice-cranes and its smoke, was to windward of us. Yes, the wind was certainly lighter here, but we should know better when the ebb had carried us through the harbour entrance.

At the entrance the sea was a mild affair after the turmoil of yesterday, but the wind was more easterly and it might prove that the shelter of Southsea was keeping things quiet here. We had our oilskins on, in readiness for a dusting.

Past the long sea-front of Southsea the yacht sailed—now in full daylight, and the lighted buoys gleamed no longer. Southsea Castle was passed, and course was shaped for the Passage Dolphins, which allow of a short cut through the line of obstructions between the Horse Fort and Southsea beach.

" No oilskins to-day, unless for rain," my companion said, as he peeled his coat off and stowed it in the cabin. The sea was much more complacent ; and so also—as events proved—was the weather. Greyness of the morning gradually melted, and the sky was cloudless blue.

The Passage Dolphins once left astern, we were really in the open once more. Beating eastward, we kept well offshore, because the sands dry out a long way seaward.

Off the entrance to Langston Harbour they can be seen at low tide—a big brown stretch of them. Even at high water it is not wise to take liberties; the sands on either side, called the West Winner and East Winner respectively, have very shallow patches, and I remember feeling my way over them one dark evening, by the lead, when entering Langston. The sudden shoaling at a spot where the sand, at low water, dries to a height of ten feet, drove me off seaward in a great hurry, I remember. Finding I could cut no corners, I kept well in the channel.

The narrow entrance to Langston, with a number of anchored barges there, was soon opened. We were not entering to-day; the helm went down and we turned seaward again. Every board carried us farther and farther from the factory chimneys and smoke of Portsmouth and the barracks of Eastney. The flat shore of Hayling Island was here instead. Broken only by a few houses and coast-guard stations and boat-sheds, the long line of it stretched onward towards the entrance.

Sunlight to south of us was a broken dazzle on the water; white sails gleamed in the sun.

"The only thing is—the sun is eating up the wind. Will the breeze last to put us inside before the tide turns?"

We had made a close fit of it, and our boards were now made right up to the beach each time in order to economise distance on the curve. The

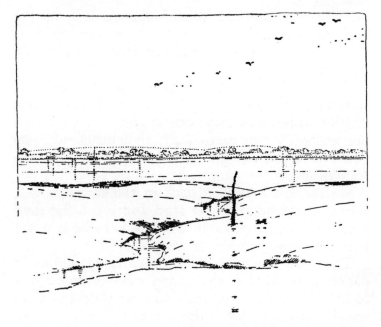

A MUD CREEK IN CHICHESTER HARBOUR

lead was kept going at the end of the landward tack. Waves, from the wind of yesterday, were still breaking in white foam over the bar and the yacht was tumbled about in the patch of broken water before, on her last board, she made the entrance, and was able to reach in, with the yellow shingle bank of Hayling Island close aboard of her. The shore is steep-to; she could sail right beside the beach.

With westerly winds, Mengham is a good anchorage, but not to-day.

" Somewhere off West Wittering is the place for

us," I said, pointing to the eastern side of the harbour entrance. "There's a spot very close to the beach, and the shelter, in an easterly wind, will be perfect."

The Stocker and Pilsey sands, inside the harbour, were completely covered; the harbour was a sheet of blue water. Just at turn of the tide, we let go our anchor. The berth was a delightful one; we could look out straight to the open sea, yet lie rock-steady.

We sat and lazed on deck in the sunshine well into the afternoon. The sand-dunes and flat sand beside us were basking in the heat; in deep water here, we were close beside the shore.

Then we landed. By quite a long curve of flat sand, seaward of the dunes, was the easiest way to West Wittering, where there are shops, and we could replenish the larder. Having shopped, we sat on the sand-dunes, looking seaward, and relapsed to our previous occupation of complete idleness. After a start at three a.m. on two days running we had earned it.

The tide was now low. In the evening, we sailed about in the dinghy among the sandbanks in the harbour, landing on the island shoals of the Stocker and Pilsey sands. While the tide came up, we stood upon narrowing islands of ribbed sea-sand, and watched them gradually diminish under that creeping and relentless rise. The sun was low in the west, and the place was a complete solitude. At dusk a few fishing boats passed us; we had no other company.

In the late twilight we went ashore again, our islands having been completely obliterated under a smooth sea—almost glassy calm. We paced over the dark-brown sand, which was as deserted as the sea. The distant Isle of Wight was a long grey outline on the grey horizon.

When we turned in the silence was complete, and the yacht lay stirless, mirrored in the calm. We awoke to a racket of noise, with the rain sweeping in torrents along the deck. The yacht was being tossed violently, and she snubbed angrily at her cable.

" Not quite so peaceful," I said with a yawn, as I awoke, heavy-eyed, just before eight.

The wind had run out to the south-west, and had breezed up strongly. With that change of wind, the yacht had lost the shelter of the shore, and the waves were running in to her straight from the sea. Little wonder now if her berth was an uneasy one.

We should be glad to get out of this ; and breakfast was a hasty affair. Then we got our anchor, with the sturdy help of the winch. One small jib made the yacht turn on her heel, and under that slip of sail she raced up the harbour, through sheets and torrents of rain that blotted everything from sight. We were even concerned lest we should pass Bosham Creek without seeing it !

At Bosham we brought up. Later in the day, when the rain had ceased, I went ashore to renew my acquaintance with the town. All these little water-side towns which are scattered about the tidal estuaries are picturesque ; but even in such company Bosham is conspicuous.

Hereabouts is an ideal cruising ground for very small yachts. They can, if they will, sail over miles of salt water and from small port to port without ever going to sea at all. All the spurs and inlets of Chichester and Langston Harbours are available in this way, for it is possible to pass from one to the other through the two swing bridges at Langston.

On the way, Emsworth can be visited, but the yacht—if staying long—must anchor below it, for the port itself dries out. *Growler* can take the bottom comfortably, but not every yacht can do the same.

The little town of Langston, before the war, was a port with its own life and business. Generally a topsail schooner was alongside with a cargo of coal or stone. Since the war its traffic has almost disappeared. The old houses nestle there by the waterside, but ships that come this way are few.

When the railway to Hayling Island was first constructed in 1867, the intention was to build docks in Sinah Lake, and to run steamers to the Isle of Wight from Hayling Island. The project came to nothing, and the railway nowadays is a very countrified affair ; but it was railways all the same that finished the sea-borne trade of Langston.

The fishing boats are the boats that remain—a quite distinct and indigenous type, the general design and rig of which has not altered for a century. Some of these open boats are of great age and have been handed down for generations from father to

BOSHAM, SUSSEX.

son.  The same type of boat is in general use in both harbours ; there are in addition larger vessels, decked, ketch-rigged, and with lee-boards.

The islands among which one sails at high water have their own history.  Langston Harbour was a favourite centre for smuggling.  The Oyster House, built on an artificial island of stone and gravel about a hundred years ago, is said to have been erected for this very purpose ; it is approached by a causeway at low water.  The house is three miles from the nearest habitation, and, surrounded by water, mud, and marshes, the place is solitude itself.  Five low-lying islands in all are dotted about the upper part of the harbour, and are known as Binnesses.  In prize-fighting days, Furse Bush Binness was a famous meeting-place for fights, the combatants being ferried over from the mainland, clear of the police.  The last fight was some time in the 'fifties.

A sea-wall about six miles long surrounds the upper part of the harbour, enclosing many hundred acres of good grazing land reclaimed from the sea. This is said to be one of the few examples of successful reclamation work undertaken by private enterprise ; the wall was built in 1820 by a local landowner, and battleship timbers were employed to shore up the chalk and stones used for it.  The whole work is still sound and good.

No doubt there was plenty of battleship wood about, for these harbours had important shipyards in their time.  Merchant vessels in plenty were built here too.  Perhaps the best-known of the

AT EMSWORTH

Chichester ships was in fact the four-masted barquentine *Transit*, built on an experimental plan. She was not altogether a failure, but was not of sufficient merit to warrant a repetition.

In a small boat it is possible to penetrate to Portsmouth Harbour at high water, through The Cut, under two fixed bridges; but this passage dries at low tide.

After many quiet hours in the two harbours, *Growler* was now to be laid up for the winter. October had come. In a mud berth at Itchenor, in Chichester Harbour, she lay stripped of her gear; and the winter went by.

In the spring-time she was brought on to the Hard at Itchenor, and there she lay for her fitting out. The trees, leafless in early April, were massed green in May; the fields were gold with the buttercups; gorse and broom were in blossom; the woods were floored with bluebells and the hedgerows white with hawthorn.

Turning out from the cabin, when the yacht was still on the shore, one's eye—many a time during the day—had lifted instinctively to the masthead to see the direction of the wind by the burgee. No burgee was there, only a mast stripped of rigging; and the deck under one's feet had the solid hardness of the shore below it.

But not now. The time had come when, even as one sat in the cabin, a subtle change was present. The lamp hanging over the table was never absolutely still; if one watched it, one could see that it was always just astir. The yacht was afloat.

There was a sense of resiliency about everything; you felt once more that she was water-borne. Summer was coming. Her sails white in the sunshine, she would now be away once more—for the long horizons of the salt blue sea.

# INDEX